GREEK HISTORICAL DOCUMENTS

GREEK HISTORICAL DOCUMENTS

THE FOURTH CENTURY B.C.

JOHN WICKERSHAM
GERALD VERBRUGGHE

HAKKERT, TORONTO
1973

Printed in the United States of America

Standard Book Numbers
   Cloth: 88866-527-X
   Paper: 88866-528-8

Library of Congress Catalogue Card Number
   73-83517

Copyright © 1973 by John Wickersham and G. P. Verbrugghe
All Rights Reserved

A. M. Hakkert Ltd., 554 Spadina Crescent
Toronto Canada M5S 2J9

FOR JOHN FINE

CONTENTS

Preface	xi
Abbreviations and Symbols	xiii

1. The Athenians Honor the Samians, 403/2 B.C. — 3
2. Decree of the State of Eleusis, 403/2 B.C. — 6
3. The Outbreak of the Corinthian War, 397-395 B.C. — 6
4. Thebes Persuades Athens to War, 395 B.C. — 17
5. Treaty of Alliance Between Athens and Boeotia, 395 B.C. — 19
6. Treaty of Alliance Between Athens and Lokris, 395 B.C. — 20
7. Treaty of Alliance Between Athens and Eretria, 394 B.C. — 21
8. Athenian Cavalry Dead in 394 B.C. — 22
9. The Stele of Dexileos, 394 B.C. — 22
10. Fortification of the Peiraieus, 394-391 B.C. — 24
11. Decree Honoring Dionysios, 393 B.C. — 25
12. Treaty of Alliance Between Amyntas and the Chalcidians, 393 B.C. — 25
13. Monetary Agreement Between Mytilene and Phokaia, Early Fourth Century B.C. — 27
14. Arbitration Between Miletos and Myus, 391-388 B.C. — 28
15. The King's Peace (The Peace of Antalkidas), 387/6 B.C. — 29
16. Phanokritos of Parion Is Publicly Honored, 386 B.C. — 33
17. Treaty of Alliance Between Athens and Chios, 384 B.C. — 34
18. Pausanias Honors His Son Agesipolis, 381/0 B.C. — 35
19. Treaty of Alliance Between Athens and Byzantium, 378/7 B.C. — 36
20. Treaty of Alliance Between Athens and Methymna, 377 B.C. — 36

21.	Thebes Joins the Second Athenian Confederacy, 378/7 B.C.	37
22.	The Decree of Aristoteles, 377 B.C.	38
23.	Treaty of Alliance Between Chalkis and Athens, 377 B.C.	40
24.	Athenian Amphictyons at Delos, 377 B.C.	41
25.	Treaty of Alliance of Corcyra, Akarnania and Kephallenia with Athens, 375 B.C.	44
26.	Treaty of Alliance Between Athens and Corcyra, 375 B.C.	45
27.	Jason of Pherai	46
28.	The Peace of 375/4 B.C.	49
29.	Treaty of Alliance Between Amyntas and Athens, 375-373 B.C.	52
30.	Athenian Navy Records, ca. 372 B.C.	53
31.	Decrees Relating to the Second Athenian Confederacy, 372 B.C.	55
32.	First Peace Treaty of 371 B.C.	56
33.	The Battle of Leuctra, 371 B.C.	58
34.	Second Peace Treaty of 371 B.C.	58
35.	Boeotia Honors the Carthaginian Nobas, Between 370 and 366 B.C.	59
36.	Thessaly Commemorates Pelopidas, 370-360 B.C.	59
37.	Athens Honors the Spartan Koroibos, 367 B.C.	60
38.	Treaty of Alliance Between Athens and Dionysios, 367 B.C.	61
39.	Athenian Complaint Against Aetolia, 367 B.C.	62
40.	Plots Against Maussollos, 367-354 B.C.	63
41.	Athenians in Samos, 365-324 B.C.	64
42.	Boeotia Honors a Byzantine, ca. 365-364 B.C.	65
43.	Contributions for Rebuilding the Temple at Delphi, 363 B.C.	66
44.	Rebellions in Ioulis, 362 B.C.	68
45.	Athens Honors Menelaos of Pelagonia, 362 B.C.	70
46.	Alliance of Athens and Peloponnesians, 362 B.C.	71
47.	Common Peace of 362 B.C.; The Stele of the Satraps	72
48.	Athens Sends Settlers to Poteidaia, 361 B.C.	73
49.	Alliance of Athens and Thessaly, 361 B.C.	73
50.	Macedon Captures Amphipolis, 357 B.C.	75
51.	Settlement Between Athens and the Kings of Thrace, 357 B.C.	76

52.	Alliance of Athens and Euboian Cities, 357/6 B.C.	77
53.	Athenian Help to Eretria, 357/6 B.C.	78
54.	The Social War: A Historian in Command at Arkesine, 357/6 B.C.	78
55.	The Social War: Andros Garrisoned, 356 B.C.	79
56.	Provisions for Keos, ca. 356 B.C.	80
57.	Athens Makes Alliance with Northern Kings, 356 B.C.	81
58.	Alliance Between Philip and Olynthos, 356 B.C.	82
59.	Athens Deals with Neapolis, 355 B.C.	83
60.	The Third Sacred War: Record of Contributions, 355-351 B.C.	84
61.	Athens Renews Monopoly on Ocher from Keos, before 350 B.C.	86
62.	Leukon Grants Trade Privileges to Mytilene, ca. 350 B.C.	87
63.	Treaty of Alliance Between Erythrai and Hermias of Atarneus, ca. 350 B.C.	88
64.	Philip Destroys Olynthos, 348 B.C.	89
65.	Athens Honors the Sons of Leukon, 346 B.C.	89
66.	Mytilene Rejoins the Second Athenian Confederacy, 346 B.C.	91
67.	Peace of Philokrates, 346 B.C.	92
68.	Accounts of the Delphian Sanctuary, 346-344 B.C.	94
69.	Speusippos' Letter to Philip, ca. 343 B.C.	97
70.	Phokis Pays Reparations for the Sacred War, 342 B.C.	101
71.	Athens Grants Privileges to Arybbas the Molossian, ca. 342 B.C.	103
72.	Athens Grants Honors to Tenedos, 339 B.C.	104
73.	Battle of Chaironeia, 338 B.C.	105
74.	Peace of 338/7 B.C.	106
75.	Athenian Law Against Tyranny, 336 B.C.	107
76.	Sicilian Treaties, 405-339 B.C.	109

Glossary	111
Tables	114

1. Athenian Eponymous Archons 403-336 B.C.
2. The Ten Athenian Tribes
3. The Twelve Athenian Months
4. Athenian and Aeginetan Money Standards
5. Spartan Kings

6. Persian Emperors
 7. Macedonian Kings
 8. Concordance of Sources
Index of Persons   119
Geographical Index   126

Plate I   Athena Greets Hera, 403-402 B.C. (see No. 1).   4
Plate II   Stele of Dexileos, 394 B.C. (see Nos. 8 and 9).   23
Plate III Eirene (Peace) and the Infant Ploutos (Wealth)
           375/4 B.C. (see No. 28).   51
Plate IV   Democracy Crowning the People of Athens, 336 B.C.
           (see No. 75).   108

PREFACE

The history of Greece in the fourth century B.C. was a continuation of the fifth century: a struggle for the hegemony of the Greeks. The hegemony finally fell to Philip of Macedon; the large political units which resulted from the Macedonian conquest of Greece and the East became the building blocks of the Hellenistic World and of the eastern Roman Empire. The pivotal period which preceded is too often handled as an afterthought of the Peloponnesian War and too often skimped in the textbooks. Our major aim in presenting these documents in translation is to illuminate the diplomatic narrative of the period covered (403-336 B.C.). All the translations are our own, and we have furnished each item with a short commentary in order to supply needed background information and narrative continuity. We hope that this collection will find use on many levels, as an introduction to direct study for beginners, as handy reference for experts.

The supporting materials are intended as quick helps to reading and as *aides-mémoire*. They are, of course, not complete discussions. The student must go elsewhere for decently circumstantial narrative. For study of the inscriptions as inscriptions, see *The Study of Greek Inscriptions* by A. G. Woodhead (Cambridge, 1959); for information on individual topics, see the separate articles in *The Oxford Classical Dictionary*. The best source for the workings of the Athenian government (the best-known ancient Greek state) is Aristotle's description (see *Aristotle's Constitution of Athens and Related Texts*, translated and annotated by K. von Fritz and E. Kapp, New York, 1950). On the complicated matter of the clan and tribe structure of Athens and other states, see

Antony Andrewes, *Greek Society* (Harmondsworth, 1971), pp. 83-96.

In transliterating Greek names and words, we have been rather "reformist," with some deference shown to established forms; our principles are essentially those employed by Professor Lewis in the preceding volume (N. Lewis, *The Fifth Century B.C.*, Toronto 1971, p. xiii). Our one notable idiosyncrasy is the use of "from" to denote the deme of an Athenian citizen, while "of" is reserved for a person's city or country.

Credits and thanks: to Dr. Dieter Ahrens of the Antikensammlung in Munich for Plate III; to Mr. B. Schmaltz of the Deutsches Archaeologisches Institut in Athens for Plates I (DAI no. A.V. 57) and II (DAI no. Ker. 5977); Plate IV is by courtesy of the American School of Classical Studies at Athens. Special thanks are owed to Michael Jameson, who read drafts of the manuscript, and to Virginia Jameson, who helped in preparing the map.

April 9, 1973.
John M. Wickersham
Ursinus College

Gerald P. Verbrugghe
Rutgers University, Camden

ABBREVIATIONS AND SYMBOLS

BCH	*Bulletin de Correspondance Hellénique.*
Bengtson	H. Bengtson, *Die Verträge der griechisch-römischen Welt von 700 bis 338 v. Chr.*, Munich 1962. In our references we give the number of the item.
Bruce	I. A. F. Bruce, *An Historical Commentary on the Hellenica Oxyrhynchia*, Cambridge, 1967.
IG	*Inscriptiones Graecae*
JHS	*Journal of Hellenic Studies.*
Lewis	N. Lewis, *Greek Historical Documents, The Fifth Century B.C.*, Toronto, 1971.
Meiggs-Lewis	R. Meiggs and D. Lewis, *A Selection of Greek Historical Inscriptions to the End of the Fifth Century B.C.*, Oxford, 1969. We give the number of the inscription.
NC	*Numismatic Chronicle.*
P. Oxy.	*The Oxyrhynchus Papyri*, ed. B. P. Grenfell and A. S. Hunt, London, 1908.
PSI	*Papiri greci e latini*, Florence, 1949.
Seltman	C. Seltman, *Greek Coins*, London, 1955.
SIG³	W. Dittenberger, *Sylloge Insriptionum Graecarum*, 3d (=4th) edn., Leipzig, 1915-1924.
Tod	M. N. Tod, *A Selection of Greek Historical Inscriptions*, 2 vols., Oxford, 1946 and 1948. We give the number of the inscription.

( ) generally enclose an editorial insertion, rather than a part of the actual text.

... always indicate a gap in the actual text, never the editors' abridgement.

GREEK HISTORICAL DOCUMENTS

1. THE ATHENIANS HONOR THE SAMIANS, 403/2 B.C.
Tod 97

Samos had been a charter member of the Delian League and had maintained her status as a supplier of ships longer than all the other dependent states except Mytilene, reduced in 428/7 B.C., and Chios, which revolted in 412/11 B.C. Samos rebelled in 441-439 B.C., causing a grave international crisis (see Thucydides 1.40.5). Her navy was taken, and a democratic government was established. Much later, when the Ionian War was pulling Athens' empire down upon her own head, Samos proved a uniquely faithful ally. Samos was the stronghold of the Athenian democracy-in-exile during the oligarchy of the Four Hundred (see Thucydides 8.72-77), and even after the disaster at Aegospotami in 405 B.C. Samos declared her willingness to resist the Spartans as long as Athens refused to surrender. Athens' grateful reply is preserved (Tod 96 = Lewis p. 41). The effects of that decree were interrupted by the surrender to Lysander and the period of the Thirty, the brutal pro-Spartan oligarchy which governed Athens until overthrown by patriots assisted by King Pausanias in 403 B.C. (see Xenophon, *Hellenica* 2.3.1-2.4.43 and Aristotle, *Constitution of Athens* 35-38). The original inscription of the decree honoring the Samians, probably destroyed by the Thirty, was re-inscribed in 403/2 B.C., together with the two new decrees which follow, confirming the previous honors and praising individual Samians. The relief on p. 4 decorated the top of the inscriptions. For later evidence of the relations between Athens and Samos see No. 41.

Decree of the Council and Assembly. Pandionis held the prytany, Agyrrhios from Kollytos was secretary, Eukleides was archon, Kallias from Oe presided, and Kephisophon made the motion. The Samians are to be publicly commended because they have been men of good-will towards the Athenians. Everything previously voted by the Athenian assembly for the people of Samos is also to be confirmed (Tod 96). The Samians may send, as they request, whomever they desire to Sparta. Since they also

Plate I Athena Greets Hera, 403-2 B.C.
(Courtesy of Deutsches Archaeologisches Institut, Athens)

ask that Athens take part, ambassadors are to be chosen to co-operate with the Samians for our benefit and to join counsel with them. Also Ephesos and Notion are to be publicly commended because they readily received the Samian exiles. The Samian embassy is to be presented to the Assembly to negotiate whatever request they have. The Samian embassy is to be invited to dine tomorrow at the Prytaneion. Kephisophon moved: in addition to the Council's recommendations the Athenians are to vote to confirm the previous measures passed concerning the Samians, just as the Council prepared and presented them to the people. The Samian embassy is to be invited to dine at the Prytaneion tomorrow.

Decree of the Council and Assembly. Erechtheis held the prytany, Kephisophon from Paiania was secretary, Eukleides was archon, Python from Kedoi presided, Eu... made the motion. Poses of Samos is to be publicly commended because he has been well-disposed towards the Athenians. In return for the good he has done the people, he is to be given 500 drachmas for the making of a crown: the Treasurers are to disburse this money. He is also to be presented to the people to receive whatever benefit they can give him. The secretary of the Council is to give him immediately a written copy of this decree. The visiting Samians are to be invited to dine at the Prytaneion tommorrow. . . . moved. In addition to the Council's recommendation Poses of Samos and his sons are to be publicly commended because they have been well-disposed towards the people of Athens. The measures previously voted by the Athenian people are to be confirmed. The secretary is to inscribe the decree on a stone stele, and the Treasurers are to furnish the money for the stele. Poses is to be given a gift of 1,000 drachmas because of his valor on behalf of Athens and a golden crown is to be made with the money. The crown is to be inscribed to say that he has been crowned for his loyalty and valor on behalf of Athens. The Samians are to be publicly commended because they have been well-disposed toward the Athenians. If they have any request to make of the people, the *prytaneis* are to present them to the people immediately after the sacrifices. The *prytaneis* are also to present the sons of Poses to the Council at the next session. Poses, his sons, and the Samians present are to be invited to dine at the Prytaneion.

2. DECREE OF THE STATE OF ELEUSIS, 403/2 B.C.
Bengtson 213

The democracy at Athens was restored in 403 B.C. The oligarchs and their supporters withdrew to Eleusis, long a part of Attica, and established a separate state. Aristotle in the *Constitution of Athens* 39 describes the arrangements which settled the relations between Athens and Eleusis (see Lewis pp. 43-45); the following inscription is believed to be a portion of those arrangements. This unnatural situation, as narrated by Xenophon in the *Hellenica* 2.4.24-43, lasted only until 401/0 B.C. when Athens captured Eleusis. Note that the inscription speaks of Athens as an ally of Sparta, as required by the peace treaty which ended the Peloponnesian War.

[The beginning is lost.]
... let the Thirty hand him over to the Two for punishment as prescribed. If the punishment is contested, let there be a trial within five days. ... Let the archons post guards to watch those who enter and leave, in order to prevent anyone from entering in violation of the decrees of the Council of Eleusis. Anyone who was residing at Eleusis before the war is a citizen of Eleusis. An Athenian may enter Eleusis just as before for the sake of the Mysteries. No foreigner or runaway may enter Eleusis without suffering the punishment prescribed. Athens may bring troops across the territory of Eleusis when Sparta summons her against the enemy ...
[The end is lost.]

3. THE OUTBREAK OF THE CORINTHIAN WAR, 397-395 B.C., BY "P"
Hellenica Oxyrhynchia, chapters VI-XXII

The Peloponnesian War was supposedly a grand act of co-operation by Sparta and her allies, intended to end Athenian power and the threat it represented to Greek security. After the war Sparta was the strongest power in Greece and felt powerful enough to attack her former ally Persia in an attempt to win back the Greeks in Asia, whom she had bargained away in the Ionian War (Thucydides 8.58): Sparta supported the rebel Cyrus in 401 B.C. and sent armies into Asia, under Thibron in 400/399, Derkyllidas in 399-397, and King Agesilaus in 397-394. In addition to alienating Persia, Sparta brought on herself a war with her allies in Greece, and this war, known as the Corinthian War (395-387 B.C.), catapulted Athens back into the center of events. Persia gave aid to the enemies of Sparta (No. 10); Corinth joined Argos, and, together with Thebes, both allied with Athens (Nos. 4 and 5).

Continuous accounts of these events survive in Xenophon, *Hellenica* 3.4-5.1 and in Didorus Siculus, Book 14. A new source for the period was published in 1908 as Oxyrhynchus Papyrus (*P. Oxy.*) 842. The name and identity of the author remain unknown. The text is referred to as the *Hellenica Oxyrhynchia* — "Greek History from Oxyrhynchus" — and the author as "The Oxyrhynchus Historian" or simply "P" (for "Papyrus author"). He seems to have been a writer of independent mind and great diligence. *P. Oxy.* 842, divided into 17 "chapters" by the editors, presented episodes in the years 397-395 B.C. Five more "chapters," dealing with the end of the Peloponnesian War (ca. 410 to ca. 406 B.C.), were published as *PSI* 1304 in 1949. All twenty-two were arranged in historical order and numbered consecutively in Bartoletti's Teubner edition; our translation is based on that edition, so that it is numbered VI-XXII. The imperfect condition of the papyrus causes considerable doubt and controversy over many details of the narrative and its precise chronology. We can point out, however, three main subjects:

Affairs in Greece (Chapter VII) from 397 B.C. leading to the beginning of the Corinthian War, with special attention to Athens (VI, VIII) and Boeotia (XVI, which outlines the Boeotian constitution, XVII-XVIII).

Conon, who was the only Athenian commander to escape the disaster at Aegospotami (Xenophon, *Hellenica* 2.1.29). Entering service with Persia, he became more and more prominent in naval affairs in the East as opposition to Sparta grew; his crowning achievement was to be the destruction of the Spartan navy near Knidos in 394 B.C. (see No. 10). In the papyrus, Conon's adventures from 396 to 395 B.C. are dealt with in chapters IX, X, XV and XIX.

Agesilaus' successful campaigns in Asia in 395 B.C., in chapters XI, XII, XIII, XXI and XXII.

For discussion of the author and his work, and a commentary on the text, see I. A. F. Bruce, *An Historical Commentary on the Hellenica Oxyrhynchia*, Cambridge, 1967.

VI Around the same time, a trireme sailed out of Athens without public authority. Its captain was Demainetos. He had, however, so they said, secretly conspired with the Council and had the collaboration of several citizens, with whom he went to the Peiraieus. Launching a ship, he sailed away from the docks and headed for Conon. An uproar followed, and the prominent upper-class politicians were enraged. They accused the Council of throwing the city into a war with Sparta; the Councillors were frightened and called an assembly. Thrasyboulos, Aisimos, Anytos and their supporters stood up and lectured them on the danger of not absolving the city of responsibility. The respectable and wealthy Athenians were not inclined to upset matters anyway, but even the masses and demagogues were on this occasion so frightened as to follow the advice. They sent to Milon, the harmost in Aigina, telling him to punish Demainetos, since he was acting without authority. Previously the masses and demagogues had spent all their time stirring up trouble and crossing the Spartans in many ways.

VII For they sent arms and crew for the ships with Conon and ambassadors to the King ... and Hagnias and Telesegoros. These were caught by the former navarch Pharax and sent off to the Spartans who executed them. Opposition (to interfering with Demainetos) was spurred by the party of Epikrates and Kephalos, for they were eager to embroil the city in war. This had been their desire even long before they had spoken with Timokrates and taken his money. Some still insist that Timokrates' money was what brought together these Athenians and the men in Boeotia and the other cities mentioned. Those who say it was the money are unaware that these men had long been hostile to the Spartans and had been on the watch for a way of getting the cities into war. The Argive and Boeotian malcontents hated the Spartans for supporting their political opponents, while the Athenians wished to rouse their country from peace and idleness and lead it into war and mischievous activity, so that they could enrich themselves at the public expense. Some of the Corinthian radicals were enemies of Sparta, just like the Boeotians and Argives. Timolaos alone had personal complaints; he had formerly been the foremost supporter of Sparta, as is clear from the events of the Decelean War. For with a fleet of five ships he plundered several Athenian islands; with two ships he sailed to Amphipolis where he acquired four more and defeated Simichos the Athenian general, as I have told above, capturing five enemy triremes and the thirty ships they were escorting. Later he sailed with triremes to Thasos and caused the island to revolt from Athens. Thus it was the individuals in the cities mentioned and their motives which account for the hostility in these cities against Sparta, not Pharnabazos and the money.

VIII Milon, the harmost at Aigina, when he heard the news

from the Athenians, quickly manned a trireme and set out after Demainetos. The latter was at that moment near Thorikos in Attica. (When attacked by Milon, Demainetos) captured one of the enemy ships. Because his own ship was in worse condition, he abandoned it after moving his crew into the captured ship and sailed on to Conon's army. Milon, having accomplished nothing, sailed back to Aigina.

IX The main events in Greece during this winter were as described: the beginning of the summer . . . the eighth year began (either 396 or 395) . . . to command the ships of the Spartans and the allies there arrived the admiral Pollis from Sparta, having been appointed as successor to Archelaidas. Meanwhile, ninety Phoenician and Cilician ships arrived at Kaunos; ten had sailed from Cilicia, while the rest . . . But Conon . . . perceiving took . . . manned the ship . . . as quickly as possible the river called Kaunios, into the Bay of Kaunos he sailed . . . of Pharnabazos and Conon . . . phernes, a Persian, . . . of affairs . . .

XI . . . hoplites and fifty light-armed, and he put the Spartiate Xenokles in command, directing that the approach . . . to form for battle. Arising with the dawn he once again led the army forward. The barbarians followed as usual, and some of them attacked the Greeks, while others rode around them and others followed in poor order along the plain. When Xenokles thought it was time to engage the enemy, he arose from his ambush and drove the Peloponnesians on at a run. As the barbarians saw the Greeks attacking they fled over the plain. When Agesilaus saw the rout he sent out from his army the light-armed and the cavalry to pursue them; and these joined the men from the ambush in pressing on the barbarians. The pursuit did not last long, since the Greeks could not catch up with the barbarians, who were mounted or otherwise unencumbered. They shot down about 600 of them and then broke off chase to attack the barbarian camp; this was not seriously guarded and they swiftly captured it. They took a large amount of provisions and many men, as well as equipment and money, some of which belonged to Tissaphernes.

XII Such was the course of the battle, and the barbarians, terrified of the Greeks, retreated to Sardis with Tissaphernes. Agesilaus remained in the area for three days, in which he returned the enemies' bodies under a truce, erected a trophy and ravaged all the land; he then led the army back into Greater Phrygia. On this march he no longer kept the army formed in a square, but allowed the men to range at will over the country so as to injure the enemy. When Tissaphernes learned that the Greeks were advancing, he gathered up his barbarians and followed at a distance of many stades. When Agesilaus had crossed the plain of Lydia he led the army ... through the mountains which lie between Lydia and Phrygia. After the passage, he brought the Greeks down until they arrived at the Maeander river. Its springs are at Kelainai, which is the greatest city of Phrygia; it empties into the sea near Priene ... Having encamped his Peloponnesians and allies, he made sacrifice to see whether or not he should cross the river and go on to Kelainai, or lead the soldiers back. Because the sacrifices were not favorable to crossing, he stayed at the river for the rest of that day and led them away on the next ...

XIII (This chapter, which seems to deal with the activities of the satraps, including the removal and execution of Tissaphernes, is too fragmented to translate.)

XIV. ... he was distinguished for the level-headedness he brought to his activities. Unlike all the former dynasts, he did not display rapacity for money and was most democratic ...

(This is apparently a favorable portrait of a contemporary head of state; for discussion of his identity, see Bruce pp. 93-96.)

XV (The scene has changed to Rhodes.) ... Each day Conon reviewed his soldiers under arms in the harbor on the pretext of preventing idleness from dulling their effectiveness against the enemy; but his intention was actually to give heart to the Rhodians with the sight of armed men ready to begin action. When he had made his usual review for all to see, he took twenty triremes and sailed to Kaunos, wishing to be absent when the governors were killed. He told his assistants Hieronymos and Nikophemos to take care of the business. These men held their hand for that day, but when the soldiers had mustered for the usual review on the next day, they led some under arms to the harbor, but stationed the rest outside the agora. When the Rhodians who were in the plot thought it was time to act, they gathered in the agora with daggers. One of them, Dorimachos, climbed up onto the stone where the heralds stand and shouted at the top of his lungs, "Citizens! Let us attack the tyrants immediately." When he had given this call for action, the others leapt with their daggers into the councils of the governors and killed the followers of Diagoras and eleven other citizens. They then held an assembly of the Rhodian people. They had just assembled when Conon returned from Kaunos with the triremes. The killers overthrew the present government and set up a democracy; they also exiled a few citizens. This was the conclusion of the revolution at Rhodes.

XVI Boeotia and Phokis went to war this summer. Certain Thebans were especially responsible for the hostilities, and behind their acts lay a faction-fight among the Boeotian politicians. At this time the government of Boeotia was as follows: each of the cities had four Councils; not all citizens could belong to them, for there was a property qualification. Each Council served in turn to initiate business and introduce it to the other three. Anything the four agreed upon became law. Such was the form of the local governments; the federal government was set up as follows: all the inhabitants of the country were divided into eleven districts, each of which provided one Boeotarch. Thebes provided four, two for the city itself and two for Plataia, Skolos, Erythrai, Skaphai and the other places which had previously merged with Thebes and were not considered her subjects. Orchomenos and Hysiai provided two Boeotarchs, Thespiai together with Eutresis and Thisbai provided two, and Tanagra provided one; Haliartos, Lebadaia, and Koroneia took turns in sending one, as also did Akraiphnia, Kopai and Chaironeia. Such, then, was the way in which the districts furnished the governors. They also provided Councilors, sixty for each Boeotarch, and paid their daily expenses. The army also was levied from the districts, each one sending approximately 1,000 hoplites and 100 cavalry. The Boeotarch, in short, was the unit by which participation in the federation was measured: the capital levies, the sending of jurors and all other benefits and disadvantages of membership were apportioned the same way. Such, then, was the government of the nation, and the federal councils of Boeotia held their sessions on the Cadmea (the acropolis of Thebes).

XVII In Thebes, then, the most eminent and powerful of the citizens, as I said before, were clashing with each other. One faction was led by Ismenias, Antitheos and Androkleidas, the other by Leontiades, Asias and Koiratadas. The party of Leontiades was pro-Spartan, while that of Ismenias was responsible for the pro-Athenian stance under which they had helped the fugitive democrats. They did not really care about the Athenians, but . . . With Theban politics standing thus, and each faction having some strength, the same conditions arose in the other cities in Boeotia. At this time the party of Ismenias and Androkleidas was a bit stronger, both in Thebes itself and in the Council of Boeotia; although previously the party of Leontiades was on top and for a long time had the city under its thumb. For, as long as the Spartans were at war with Athens and carrying on at Decelea and keeping their alliance well together, then the latter party was by far the most influential, because, on one hand, the Spartans were so close, and, on the other, Thebes was receiving great benefits from this policy. Their prosperity was much increased . . . as soon as the Peloponnesian War began. For when Athens began to fight Boeotia, the people of Erythrai, Skaphai, Skolos, Aulis, Schoinos, Potniai and many other places which had no walls, merged themselves with Thebes, thus doubling her territory. The Thebans did especially well out of their participation in the Decelea operations, because they bought up slaves and other booty at very low prices, and, being neighbors of Attica, they moved all its capital into Boeotia, starting with the wood and tiles of the houses. Attica was then the best-developed part of Greece; it had suffered but little from the previous invasions, and the Athenians so managed it and worked so hard on its improvement, . . . the Thebans moved the things taken in the war from the Greeks into their own estates. The state of things in 395, however, was the following:

XVIII The party of Androkleidas and Ismenias were doing all they could to provoke a war with Sparta. They wanted to destroy Sparta's empire and prevent Sparta from helping the other party, which was friendly to Sparta, in its efforts to destroy themselves. They reckoned this would be easy, counting on money from Persia, as the envoy promised, and on the participation of Corinth, Argos and Athens, whose anti-Spartan citizens would collaborate. Their calculations led them to expect that it would be difficult to attack directly and openly; they could never persuade Thebes or the rest of Boeotia to war against Sparta, who then controlled

Greece. They proceeded to provoke a war in the following underhanded manner: they persuaded certain Phokians to invade West Lokris, on the basis of the following hostility: these two countries have a dispute over a piece of land around Parnassos. They had warred over it in times past; it had been farmed by Phokis and Lokris in turn, and when the other side discovered this was happening it would invade and steal the sheep. Previously they settled these incidents by arbitration, but this time the Lokrians just went and stole more sheep in retaliation. The Phokians immediately invaded Lokris under arms, and the friends of the party of Androkleidas and Ismenias spurred them on. The Lokrians, seeing their land wasted, sent ambassadors to Boeotia to accuse Phokis and ask for help; for Lokris was then friendly to Boeotia. The radical party immediately seized their chance and persuaded the Boeotians to help Lokris. The Phokians, when they heard about this, withdrew from Lokris and sent ambassadors to Sparta asking them to forbid the Boeotians to invade Phokis. Sparta, although not trusting what the Phokians said, nevertheless sent to Boeotia and forbade her to make war against Phokis: they said that any complaint should be brought before the Allies for arbitration. The Thebans, however, under the influence of the radicals, sent the Spartan embassy away with nothing accomplished; and the Thebans mobilized and marched against Phokis. They invaded, plundered Parapotamia and mounted attacks on Daulis and Phanotea. They withdrew from Daulis unsuccessful and with some loss, but they captured the suburbs of Phanotea. They advanced further into Phokis, overrunning most of the plain of Elatea and driving away the inhabitants of Pedia. Withdrawing by way of Hyampolis, they decided to try to take it. It is a strong position; attacking the walls with all eagerness, they accomplished nothing and lost about eighty soldiers. They then completed their withdrawal, having done the damage described above to the Phokians.

XIX When Cheirikrates, who succeeded Pollis as admiral, had taken over the Spartan and allied ships, Conon manned twenty triremes, set sail from Rhodes and went to Kaunos. From Kaunos he journied inland to Pharnabazos and Tithraustes, wishing to get money from them. At this time many months' pay was owed to the troops, and they were being let out miserably for hire by their generals. This is quite usual when one is fighting for the King; indeed, during the Decelean War, when the Persians were allies of Sparta, they were simply wretched and stingy at providing money, and many times the allied fleet would have been ruined had it not been for the zeal of Cyrus. The King is to blame: whenever he starts a war he sends his commanders a small amount of money to start with and then forgets about them altogether. His lieutenants cannot pay for everything out of their own pockets and must frequently stand by and watch their forces ruined. Such, then, is the normal situation of the King's armies. When Conon arrived and said that the situation was on the point of being lost owing to the lack of funds, he addressed men who found it unseemly to reject comrades in the King's War; and Tithraustes sent some of his barbarians with 220 talents of silver to pay the soldiers. This money was taken from the estate of Tissaphernes. Tithraustes then remained a short time in Sardis before traveling up to the King; he appointed Ariaios and Pasiphernes as generals to look after affairs and gave them the remaining money to manage the war. This money is said to have been about 700 talents.

XX The Cyprians who had sailed with Conon to Kaunos had been convinced by some wicked rumors that the money was not to be paid to them, but would merely be used to square accounts with the crews and the marines. Vexed by this thought they held an assembly and chose a man from Karpasia as their general, giving him a bodyguard made up of two men from each squad . . . . Conon insisted that everyone would receive his fair share of the money and said that he wanted to repeat this answer to the rest as well. The Cyprian general from Karpasia followed Conon to where the soldiers were concentrated. This man thus set out with Conon and when they arrived at the gates, Conon, being in the lead, went through first; but the man from Karpasia was seized at the exit by some of the Messenians who usually escorted Conon. They did this without the advice of Conon, because they wished to detain the man in the city and punish him for his misdeeds. The Cyprian escorts laid hold of him on the other side and prevented the Messenians from leading him away; the rest of the Cyprian forces had also seen the scuffle and were running to the rescue. Conon . . . leapt into the men . . . into the city. The Cyprians mounted a barrage that drove back the Messenians and then, convinced that

Conon had fabricated the whole affair about the distribution of the pay, they entered the ships intending, as some said, to take the men from Rhodes and sail to Cyprus. ...Under their urging, Conon approached Leonymos, the infantry captain. He told him that he alone could now save the King's projects. If, he said, Leonymos would give him the Greek guards who were guarding Kaunos and as many Carians as possible, then he would stop the uproar in the camp. Leonymos directed him to take as many soldiers as he wanted. Because it was near sundown, he let that day pass; but before the next dawn, taking many of Leonymos' Carians and all of the Greeks, he led them out of the city. He next stationed some outside the camp itself, while the rest ... he placed by the ships and the shore. Having commanded the herald to summon each soldier to take his post, he seized the Karpasian and sixty other Cyprians; he killed the men and crucified the general.... The men left behind in Rhodes were incensed when they heard about this, and they turned on Conon's lieutenants, driving them under fire out of the camp; then they left the harbor and spread terror and confusion among the Rhodians. When Conon arrived from Kaunos he arrested and killed their leaders and held payday for the rest. In this way, then, the King's army gravely endangered itself, but stopped its disorders because of Conon and his zeal.

XXI Agesilaus had made his way to the Hellespont with the Spartan and allied armies. As long as he was marching through Lydia he did no damage to the residents, because he wished to preserve the truce he had made with Tithraustes. But when he had reached the country of Pharnabazos, he began to ravage and plunder the land as he advanced. When he had passed the area known as the Plain of Thebe and Apia, he entered Mysia and approached the Mysians, directing them to march with him. Most of the Mysians are in fact autonomous and independent of the King. Agesilaus protected those Mysians who chose to join his expedition, but devastated the land of those who refused. When he had gotten well into the middle of the country to the so-called Mysian Olympos, he saw that the passage was narrow and dangerous; he therefore sent men to the Mysians and made a treaty with them before leading the army through. They let pass the ... of the Peloponnesians and the allies, but attacked the rearguard with missiles ... the soldiers being in poor order because of the narrowness of the area. Agesilaus collected the army and did nothing for that day, while he performed the usual services for the dead; about fifty soldiers had been killed. On the next day he set up an ambush manned by the mercenaries called "Derkyllideans," before breaking camp and getting the army back into march. All the Mysians thought that Agesilaus would depart because of the previous day's beating, and so they left their villages to pursue him, apparently intending to harry his rear as before. When, however, they came up to the ambush, the Greeks leapt out and closed with the enemy. The front ranks of the pursuing Mysians fell in quickly with the Greeks and died, but most saw their leaders enmeshed and fled back to the villages. When Agesilaus heard of the engagement, he wheeled the army back on up the road until he rejoined the ambush. He then made camp in the same place as the day before. Afterwards, the relatives of the dead Mysians sent heralds . . . and took back the bodies under truce; more than 130 died. Agesilaus took guides from the villages and led the army forward after a few days' rest. He brought them down into Phrygia, not into the same region as last summer, but into an unravaged area, which he now began to destroy. As guides he had Spithridates and his son. This Spithridates was a Persian by birth, had lived with and attended Pharnabazos. They became enemies, however, and Spithridates had fled to Kyzikos fearing arrest and ill-treatment. Later he came to Agesilaus with his son Megabates, who was a handsome youth. Agesilaus took them on board mainly because of Megabates, and he was said to have a mighty passion for the boy. He also thought that Spithridates would be a good guide and otherwise useful to the army. For these reasons, then, he gladly accepted them. Leading the army ever on and wasting the country of Pharnabazos, he arrived at a place called Lionheads. After making a few unsuccessful attacks on it, he led on again, wasting and pillaging the unharmed territory. He came again to Gordion, which is founded upon a mount and well equipped for defense. Gathering the army together, he stayed six days, in which he both attacked the enemy and allowed his soldiers some ease. The zeal of Rhathenes, the Persian commandant, prevented him from capturing the place, and so he led the soldiers inland, ordering Spithridates to lead them into Paphlagonia.

XXII He next led the Peloponnesians and the allies towards the mountains of Phrygia and Paphlagonia. He encamped there and sent Spithridates to Gyes; Spithridates made the journey, persuaded Gyes and returned with the man. Agesilaus made a treaty and led the army quickly out of Paphlagonia to the sea, fearing that winter would starve them. He did not use the same road as before, but another leading through the less tiring Sangarion. Gyes sent him . . . about 1,000 cavalry and over 2,000 infantry. When he had brought the army to Mysian Kios, he remained there six days ravaging the country of the Mysians in order to pay them back for their treachery upon Olympos; then he led the Greeks through coastal Phrygia. Here he came upon the impregnable place called Miletos' Wall, from which he led the army on. Travelling along the Rhyndakos River, he arrived at the Bay of Daskylis, the site of Daskyleion, an extremely strong royal fortress where all Pharnabazos' silver and gold was said to be stored. Agesilaus encamped the soldiers there and sent for Pankalos, who was one of Cheirikrates' adjutants and had sailed up to look after the Hellespont with five triremes. Pankalos arrived quickly and sailed into the bay with his triremes. Agesilaus ordered him to load on the most valuable booty and carry it to the . . . at Kyzikos as pay for the army. He dismissed the troops from Mysia, telling them to return in spring. He himself prepared to go to Cappadocia, hearing that this country was like a headband stretched out from the Black Sea to Cilicia and Phoenicia and was of such a size that, marching from Sinope . . .

4. THEBES PERSUADES ATHENS TO WAR, 395 B.C.
Xenophon, *Hellenica* 3.5.8-15

Thebes' attack on Phokis (No. 3, XVIII) opened the Corinthian War. Sparta reacted quickly by sending Lysander to lead the Central Greeks against Boeotia, and he was immediately successful in causing Orchomenos to revolt. Thebes now acted with urgency to secure the help of Athens and bring about a general uprising against Sparta's domination of Greece. According to Xenophon the Theban appeal to Athens was embodied in the following speech. It is extremely unlikely that the speech is a real document except in its most general aspects (see F. W. Walbank, *Speeches in Greek Historians*, Oxford, 1967). It is still, however, valuable as the historian's contemporary representation of a current outlook on the international situation, properly partisan and somewhat inaccurate. Lysander's decarchies, for example, spoken of as current grievances in section 13 of the speech, had actually been removed some years before.

It is not right, Athenians, to blame us for the atrocious measures voted against you at the end of the war. Our city did not vote for those measures; they were proposed by one man, who happened to be our representative among the allies at that time. When, by contrast, the Spartans summoned us against Peiraieus, the whole city voted against marching with them. Because it is chiefly on your account that Sparta is angry with us, we believe you ought to help our city.

We also think that those of you who were in the city ought to be especially willing to attack the Spartans, who gave you an oligarchy, made you hated by the people, arrived with a great force as if they were your allies and then betrayed you to the people. As far as they were concerned you were dead men, but the people saved you.

We all know well, Athenians, that you would like to recover your former empire. How are you more likely to achieve this than by coming to the rescue of Sparta's victims? Do not be afraid of the fact that they have many subjects. Let this rather be an encouragement, realizing that, when you had the most subjects, then also you had the most enemies. As long as they had no way of revolt they hid their hatred of you: but when Sparta became their champion, then they showed what they thought of you.

So it is now. If you and we publicly cast our shield in Sparta's face, then those who hate her will show themselves in great number. A brief reckoning will show the truth of my words. Does anyone remain well-disposed towards her? The Argives are always hostile to Sparta, are they not?

Elis certainly, robbed of much land and many cities, has been added to the list of Sparta's foes. Why even bother to mention Corinth, Arcadia or Achaia? In the war against you they were seduced into sharing all the toil, danger, and expense; but when Sparta attained her goal, what share did she give them of command, honor, or money? The Spartans decided rather to appoint Helots as harmosts, and their success has unmasked them as despots over their free allies. Your own subject cities who revolted have also surely been flagrantly swindled. Instead of freedom they got a double dose of slavery and are tyrannized by the harmosts and decarchies which Lysander established in all the cities. And the King of Persia, who contributed the most to their victory over you, what difference has it made to him which side he helped win?

Is it not, then, likely that by championing those who are so openly abused, you will become the greatest state ever known? When you had your empire you ruled only the maritime cities; now, however, you might command everyone — us, the Peloponnesians, your former subjects and the Persian King himself, who is the greatest power of all. We were, as you well know, valuable allies to the Spartans. The present situation makes it likely that we will be stauncher allies to you than we were to Sparta, because we are not, as then, coming to aid islanders, Syracusans or other foreigners, but our own injured selves.

You should also realize that Sparta's overextended empire will be far easier to destroy than was your own empire, because you were a naval power ruling over people without a fleet, whereas the Spartans, few in number themselves, are practicing their greed upon people who are many times their number and are no less well armed. There is our case. Make no mistake, Athenians; we believe that our summons will benefit you even more than us.

5. TREATY OF ALLIANCE BETWEEN ATHENS AND BOEOTIA, 395 B.C.
Tod 101

Athens was convinced by the Theban case (No. 4) and joined in a four-power coalition (Athens, Boeotia, Corinth and Argos) against Sparta. The following inscription records the resulting alliance between Athens and Boeotia. Before this treaty an alliance "without time-limit" is seen only in the treaty between Sybaris and the Serdaioi in the years 550-525 B.C. (Meiggs-Lewis 10) and has been restored in the Athenian treaties with

Rhegion in 433/2 B.C. (Meiggs-Lewis 63 = Lewis, pp. 19-20) and Leontinoi in 433/2 B.C. (Meiggs-Lewis 64). This inscription furnishes a good example of the standard form for the alliances of this period, which are defensive in their terms (technically *epimachiai*). Earlier alliances (technically *symmachiai*) tended to be offensive as well by adding that the two parties would "have the same friends and enemies."

Gods.

Alliance without time-limit between Boeotia and Athens. If anyone attacks the Athenians with warlike intent by land or sea, the Boeotians will give aid in all possible strength, as the Athenians may request. And if anyone attacks the Boeotians with warlike intent by land or sea, the Athenians will give aid in all possible strength, as the Boeotians may request. If Athens and Thebes decide in joint deliberation on any addition to or change in the existing treaty, it shall be valid. . . .

[The rest is lost.]

6. TREATY OF ALLIANCE BETWEEN ATHENS AND LOKRIS, 395 B.C.
Tod 102

Lysander was killed in attacking Haliartos shortly after his success at Orchomenos. King Pausanias, now arriving late with the Peloponnesian army, found the situation unfavorable and withdrew under truce from Boeotia (see No. 18). Sparta thus lost the head start she had gained in the War, and the anti-Spartan coalition was able to devote the winter of 395/4 B.C. to organization and enlistment of additional allies, including Lokris and Euboia (No. 7). For a complete list of the whole coalition see Diodorus Siculus 14.82.

More than one state in Central Greece was called Lokris (see map). It is likely enough that the Lokris of this inscription was the same Lokris that had furnished the *casus belli* (No. 3, XVIII), but it still remains unsure exactly which Lokris that was. See Bruce, *Commentary* pp. 118-19 for discussion of this point.

[The beginning is lost.]

. . . on the same terms as Corinth and Boeotia. Alliance without time-limit between Athens and Lokris. If anyone attacks the Athenians with warlike intent by land or sea, the Lokrians shall give aid in all possible strength, as the Athenians may request. And if anyone attacks the Lokrians with warlike intent by land or sea, the Athenians shall give aid in all possible strength, as the Lokrians may request. If Athens and Lokris agree in joint deliberation on some alteration of the treaty, it shall be valid.

7. TREATY OF ALLIANCE BETWEEN ATHENS AND ERETRIA, 394 B.C.
Tod 103

Euboean Eretria was one of the leaders in the Archaic wave of Greek colonization. She was defeated by neighboring Chalkis in the Lelantine War, one of the few known events of early Greek history. The only cities from Greece to help the Ionians in their revolt from Darius (499-494 B.C.) were Athens and Eretria. Both were attacked during Darius' retaliatory probe into Greece in 490 B.C. Athens fought Darius' attack off by the victory at Marathon, but Eretria had fallen and been destroyed. Euboia as a whole was a tightly-held part of the Athenian empire; Eretria was resettled by Athenians after the Euboean revolt of 446 B.C., but revolted again with the rest of Euboia in 411 B.C. Eretria is rather late (midsummer 394 B.C.) in joining the coalition.

Alliance between Eretria and Athens.

Decree of the Council. Akamantis held the prytany, Chelonion, son of Theo ..., was secretary, in the archonship of Euboulides (394/3), ... presided, Gnathios made the motion. Athens and Eretria will be allies ... in all possible strength. If the two cities in common deliberation decide on some improvement in the treaty, it will be valid. Athens will swear through her generals, the Council and the knights; Eretria through her generals, Council, knights and the other magistrates. ... Each shall swear its own traditional oath. The Council is to select immediately ten men, five from the Council and five private citizens, to receive the oaths from the Eretrians ...

[The end is lost.]

8. ATHENIAN CAVALRY DEAD IN 394 B.C.
Tod 104

The coalition took the offensive in the spring of 394 B.C. In Central Greece the Spartan strongpoints, Pharsalos and Herakleia, were captured, and the army of Phokis was immobilized. In summer the confederates gathered at Corinth intending to invade Laconia (see Xenophon, *Hellenica* 4.2.11-12), but this was foiled by Sparta's quick action in mobilizing and gathering the Peloponnesian army in a swift march to the Isthmus. Sparta defeated her enemies in the Battle of the Nemea (also called the Battle of Corinth, Xenophon, *Hellenica* 4.2.13-23) and discouraged them from repeating such attempts. Meanwhile, Sparta had summoned Agesilaus to drop his Asian campaigns and return to the urgent situation in Greece. Marching across the North he forced his way through hostile Thessaly and late in the summer of 394 B.C. fought the Battle of Koroneia against the army of the coalition. The battle was a victory for Agesilaus, but a side-thrust into Lokris failed, and he gained no strategic position for effective action in Central Greece. He withdrew into the Peloponnese, and all subsequent land actions of the War centered about Corinth.

The following horsemen died at Corinth:

Phylarchos, Antiphanes,
Melesias, Onetorides, Lysitheos, Pandios, Nikomachos,
Theangelos, Phanes, Demoklees, Dexileos, Eudelos.

At Koroneia:

Neokleides.

9. THE STELE OF DEXILEOS, 394 B.C.
Tod 105

This young Athenian noble, portrayed triumphant on the stele illustrated on p. 23, was mentioned in No. 8. The significance of "The Five Riders" is unknown.

Dexileos, son of Lysanias of Thorikos,
born in the archonship of Teisandros (414/3),
died in the archonship of Euboulides (394/3)
at Corinth, one of the Five Riders.

Plate II Stele of Dexileos, 394 B.C.
(Courtesy of Deutsches Archaeologisches Institut, Athens)

10. FORTIFICATION OF THE PEIRAIEUS, 394-391 B.C.
Tod 107

In the fifth century Athens based her security on her naval power and the fortifications of the city, the harbors of the Peiraieus and the Long Walls between. The peace-terms of 404 B.C. had stipulated the elimination of Athens' fleet and the destruction of the Long Walls and the Peiraieus walls. These were torn down, wrote Xenophon in *Hellenica* 2.2.23, "with great eagerness amid the sound of flutes, for people believed that this day was the beginning of freedom for Greece." As we have seen (No. 4), Athens was pressed back into a position of influence.

Shortly before the Battle of Koroneia (August 394 B.C.), the Athenian Conon led a Persian-supported fleet to a decisive victory against the Spartan navy near Knidos. Conon and the satrap Pharnabazos followed up the victory by liberating Greek cities of the Asian coast and the islands from Spartan governors and attempting to drive Sparta from the Hellespont. In the spring they took the fleet to Greece, where they ravaged the coast of Laconia, occupied Kythera and met the coalition at Corinth to encourage continued opposition to Sparta. Pharnabazos furnished a generous subsidy and permitted Conon to take the fleet to Athens along with more money to rebuild the fortifications of Athens. There is no doubt that Conon's arrival greatly pushed the work forward; but the work had actually begun even before the Battle of Knidos, as shown by *A* of the following. Xenophon (*Hellenica* 4.8.10) mentions Boeotians as helpers, referred to in *B*.

A

In the archonship of Diophantos (395/4), month Skirophorion (ca. June 395), payments for day-work: hire of teams to haul stone — 160 drachmas; hire of iron tools — 53 drachmas.

B

In the archonship of Euboulides (394/3), (payment for building) from the mark to the facade of the gates which are by the sanctuary of Aphrodite on the right as one leaves — 750 drachmas. The contractor for the transport and laying of the stones was Demosthenes the Boeotian.

11. DECREE HONORING DIONYSIOS, 393 B.C.
Tod 108

The year 393 B.C. was one of heavy diplomatic activity for Athens, beginning with the following attempt to flatter Dionysios the tyrant of Syracuse into at least giving up his alliance with Sparta. After Conon's return to Athens (see No. 10), he had an embassy sent to Dionysios which was, according to Lysias (19.19), successful in persuading Dionysios not to send triremes to aid Sparta. Dionysios, however, did furnish Sparta with twenty triremes for the crucial operations of 387 B.C. (see No. 15).

Other diplomacy in 393 B.C. included similar honors for Evagoras of Salamis (see Tod 109), and the re-establishment of Athenian amphictyons at Delos (see *IG* II^2 1634; Kupry, *BCH* 62, p. 40; and No. 24).

The Dionysios-inscription presents the earliest epigraphical example of a decree with numbered prytany, a great help in dating more precisely fourth century inscriptions.

In the archonship of Euboulides (394/3), with Pandionis holding the sixth prytany (January/February 393), when Platon son of Nikochares of Phlya was secretary.

Decree of the Council, Kinesias moved: Concerning the report of Androsthenes: Dionysios, the governor of Sicily, and Leptines, the brother of Dionysios, and Thearides, the brother of Dionysios, and Polyxenos, the brother-in-law of Dionysios, . . . are to be publicly commended . . .

[The rest is lost.]

12. TREATY OF ALLIANCE BETWEEN AMYNTAS AND THE CHALCIDIANS, 393 B.C.
Tod 111

The concept of the *polis*, the city-state, had not entered Macedon by the fourth century B.C. Its government, to speak anachronistically, was feudal: a king, approved by the nobles, ruled; they were to defend the land for the peasant farmers or herders who supported this "feudal" government with gifts in kind. Macedon in 393/2 B.C., the date of this inscription, was very small, ringed by more powerful neighbors: to the south, Thessaly; to the east, the Chalcidian League and Amphipolis, a free Greek city controlling the Strymon valley; to the north-east, north and west, the barbarian kingdoms of the Thracians, Gaetae and Illyrians. To survive as an independent small kingdom it had to ally with its neighbors against other neighbors and enter into the balance of power. In the inscription below, Amyntas III, having recently succeeded to the throne, enters into a defensive alliance with the Chalcidian League. The Illyrians were invading the west of Amyntas' kingdom; he had to secure his eastern frontier. He offers important concessions to the League, opening his kingdom with its timber resources to Chalcidian business men. He does try to retain some control over his timber, vital to those dependent upon sea power, such as Sparta (now) and Athens. The League, besides trade advantages, also secured its western boundary and would now be free to contend with Amphipolis which the League coveted, as did so many other states.

Amyntas, after this treaty was concluded, was driven from his kingdom by the Illyrians and, perhaps to ensure that his ally would live up to its defensive treaty obligations as stated in this inscription, ceded some land to the League (Diodorus Siculus 14.92.3). Amyntas was able to regain his kingdom, whether with or without the help of his ally is unknown, but soon he had difficulties with the League on the resettlement of their common boundary. They were soon at war with each other (Xenophon, *Hellenica* 5.2.12).

[Obverse]

Alliance with Amyntas, the son of Erridaios.

Alliance between Amyntas, the son of Erridaios, and the Chalcidians.

They are to be allies of each other in the eyes of all men for fifty years. If anyone invades the territory of Amyntas or of the Chalcidians, the Chalcidians will aid Amyntas and Amyntas will aid the Chalcidians.

[Reverse]

The Chalcidian League may export pitch and all types of construction timber (from Macedon) with the exception of pine wood suitable for ship timber. However, even ship timber, if the League does not need it, may be exported, provided that Amyntas is informed before its actual exportation and the prescribed export duties are paid. The League and Macedon may export and transport all other types of goods if duty is paid: by the Chalcidians to Macedon if they export or transfer goods from Macedon; by Macedon to the Chalcidians if it exports or transfers goods from the territory of the Chalcidians. Neither Amyntas nor the League without the consent of the other party may make an alliance with Amphipolis, Akanthos, Mende or the Bottiaians. Macedon and the League, if they are in agreement and deem it beneficial, may ally in common with these people. The oath of the alliance is as follows: I will keep the agreement reached by the Chalcidians and if anyone invades Amyntas' territory, I will aid Amyntas . . .

[The rest is lost.]

13. MONETARY AGREEMENT BETWEEN MYTILENE AND PHOKAIA, EARLY FOURTH CENTURY
Tod 112

Electrum ("gold" in the following inscription) coins of Lesbos and Phokaia from 480 to 350 B.C. are so similar as to suggest the long existence of a monetary agreement between the cities. The following inscription, roughly dated on epigraphic grounds to the early fourth century, may thus represent a renewal or revising of a pre-existing convention (see Seltman, *Greek Coins*, London, 1955, pp. 113-14). Found at Mytilene, it is in the Aeolic dialect.

Another monetary agreement of this period more closely concerns the diplomatic picture: the appearance of coinage from Byzantium, Ephesos, Samos, Knidos, Iasos, Kyzikos and Rhodes, all bearing an obverse showing Heracles strangling the serpents (a Theban motif) with the legend ΣΥΝ (for *synmachikon*, "coinage of the alliance"), seems to point to the formation in this area of an anti-Spartan League, surely the result of Conon's campaigns (see Seltman pp. 157-58; Cawkwell, *NC* 1956, pp. 69 ff.; and Cawkwell, *JHS* 1963, pp. 152 ff.).

[The beginning is lost.]

. . . whatever both cities . . . write on the stele or erase, it shall be valid. Anyone who debases the gold shall be subject to prosecution in both cities. In Mytilene a majority of the court will consist of the magistrates; in Phokaia the majority of the court will consist of the magistrates. The trial will take place within six months from the end of (the offender's) term of office. If he debased the gold willingly, he will be punished with death; if he is acquitted of deliberate wrongdoing, let the court decide what he will suffer or pay. The city will be held blameless and immune. Mytilene was assigned by lot to mint the first issue. This agreement takes effect under the successor of Kolonos as *prytanis* (in Mytilene) and the successor of Aristarchos (as *prytanis*) in Phokaia.

14. ARBITRATION BETWEEN MILETOS AND MYUS, 391-388 B.C.
Tod 113

According to Tod this inscription is "the earliest extant epigraphical example of an interstate arbitration in the Greek world." It records the settlement of a boundary dispute between Miletos and Myus, neighbors on the Maeander Delta, by a board of arbitrators (listed by city) from the cities of Ionia. The case was judged by Strouses (called Strouthas in the literary sources), satrap of the area 391-388 B.C.

[The beginning is fragmentary.]
... Dionys ... satrap ... disputed over the land in the Plain of the Maiandros ... become ... dispute ... of the city ... to the King and ... Strouses in order that the Ionians assemble ... (Here follow the names of the arbitrators.) *Erythraians*: ...aneos, Dicholeos, son of Pedieus, ... son of Apollas, ... Epikrates, son of A..., Pythes, son of Anakritos. *Chians*: Sostratos, son of Kleinias, Angeles, son of Hipponax, Ktesippos, son of Eoptolemos, Phanon, son of Hermomachos, Alexandros, son of Hikesias. *Klazomenians*: Isthmerios, son of Theombrotos, Artemon, son of Apollonios, Athenagores, son of Polyarchos, Zenis, son of Euandros, Herogeiton, son of Anaxitimos. *Lebedians*: Nymphodoros, son of Kallias, Aristippides, son of ..., Deiklos, son of Apollonios, Kleinias, son of Hegesion, Demokrates, son of Egdelos. *Ephesians*: Polykles, son of Theudoros, Pythokleides, son of Dionysios, Euermos, son of Athenaios, Euaion, son of Hermias, Theudoros, son of Herakleides.

The suit was joined between Miletos and Myus; the witnesses had given their testimony for both sides, the boundaries of the land had been delineated, and when the arbitrators were about to render their verdict, Myus abandoned the suit. The advocates have recorded the following as their witness to the proceedings and presented it to the arbitrating cities. Whereas Myus has abandoned the suit, Strouses, satrap of Ionia, has listened to the Ionian arbitrators and confirmed Miletos' possession of the land. Advocates for Miletos were Nymph ..., Baton, son of Diokle ...

[The rest is lost.]

15. THE KING'S PEACE (THE PEACE OF ANTALKIDAS), 387/6 B.C.
Bengtson 242

After the Battle of Koroneia, as noted above (No. 8), land operations were largely confined to the area of Corinth. In 393 B.C. Corinthian landowners pressed for peace, when their land was ravaged by Spartan marauders. The landowners were savagely repressed, and Corinth was now actually united with and run by her neighbor Argos (Xenophon, *Hellenica* 4.4.1-6; G. T. Griffith, "The Union of Corinth and Argos," *Historia* 1, 1950, pp. 236-56). Sparta succeeded in surrounding Corinth and about this same time was also successful in persuading the satrap Tiribazos to support Sparta against Athens. Athens came to the relief of Corinth and lifted the blockade. The year 392 B.C. ended with two unsuccessful peace conferences at Sardis (Xenophon, *Hellenica* 4.8.12-15) and at Sparta (see Andocides *On the Peace*). Hostilities in 391 B.C. brought a second blockade of Corinth and a second Athenian rescue. The war in Greece stabilized.

Naval events led to the war's end. King Artaxerxes had not favored Tiribazos' pro-Spartan stance and replaced him with Strouthas (see No. 14). Sparta, however, used Tiribazos' money to launch a small fleet in 390 B.C., which captured Knidos and Samos. In this year Athens took the fateful step of allying with Evagoras of Salamis who had become hostile to Artaxerxes. Athens campaigned successfully at sea under Thrasyboulos from Steiria in 389 and Iphikrates in 388/7 B.C., but in 388 B.C. Artaxerxes sent Tiribazos back to help Sparta. With Persian help the Spartan Antalkidas was able to capture the Hellespont, thus cutting off Athens' food supply as Lysander had done in 405 B.C.

The chief combatants, in their several ways, were now ready for peace. This Peace in form and execution proved extremely influential over the following half-century. It provoked resentment because: Persia had drafted the terms; it confirmed Persian ownership of the Asiatic Greeks; and Sparta apparently exploited the Peace to her own benefit (see Nos. 17-23). On the other hand, whenever afterwards the Greeks made peace on their own initiative, they preserved the essential terms of the "Peace sent down by the King" or "The Common Peace" — demobilization and autonomy.

Although Sparta held the upper hand at the time of the Peace and for some years after, the Corinthian War was clearly successful in destroying the position Sparta had gained from the Peloponnesian War: her naval empire was ruined, and her allies wavered in their allegiance; Athens had succeeded in repudiating the subjection forced upon her by the peace terms of 403 B.C., as she had her fortifications back and could once more have a navy.

Terms and Execution of the Peace

Decree of the Persian Emperor Artaxerxes

Xenophon, *Hellenica* 5.1.31: King Artaxerxes deems it just that the cities in Asia and the islands Klazomenai and Cyprus belong to him; that the other Greek cities both large and small be left autonomous, except for Lemnos, Imbros and Skyros which are to belong as of old to Athens. If either side rejects this Peace, I will make war upon him in concert with those who do accept it, by land and by sea, with ships and with money.

Diodorus Siculus 14.110.3: The King dictated the conclusion of peace on the following terms: the Greek cities in Asia were made subject to the King, but all other Greek cities were autonomous; he would act through those who accepted the terms to attack those who rejected the treaty.

Justin 6.6.1: Meanwhile, Artaxerxes, the King of Persia, sent to Greece envoys through whom he commanded all to lay down arms; anyone who refused would be treated as an enemy; and he restored to the cities their liberty and property.

Execution of the Terms

Xenophon, *Hellenica* 5.1.35-36: When these things had been done, and the cities had sworn to abide by the Peace which the King had sent down, then were the land forces disbanded and the sea forces as well. Thus was struck the first peace treaty among the Spartans, the Athenians and their allies since the beginning of the war which followed the razing of Athens' walls. The Spartans, who had just held their own in the war, gained distinction from this Peace, which is called "The Peace of Antalkidas," because they became champions of the Peace which the King had sent down and worked for autonomy in the cities. They thus recovered Corinth as an ally and made, as they had long wanted to do, the Boeotian cities autonomous from Thebes. They stopped Argos from appropriating Corinth by threatening a war if Argos did not evacuate Corinth.

Contemporary Reactions

Isocrates

Panegyrikos 176: ... commands, not a treaty. 179 f.: ... the treaty was not made before men. And he forced us to inscribe the treaty on stone tablets and set them up in the common sanctuaries.

Peace 68 (see also 115, 120, 128, 137): ... we did not cease making war until the Spartans were willing to make the treaty which featured autonomy.

Peace 16: ... the treaty with Sparta and the King, which commanded the Greeks to be autonomous, all foreign garrisons to leave the cities, and all property to be restored to each.

Panegyrikos 106-7: ... they made the Peace. No one could show that any peace treaty more shameful has ever been made, or more scornful of Greece, or more contrary to the reputation which Spartan courage has in many quarters ... Sparta betrayed many Greeks to the King. They wrote in black and white that all the Greeks in Asia were his to use as he wished ... 107: They inscribed this sort of treaty in their sanctuaries and compelled their allies to do the same.

Panathenaikos 59: ... during the period of Spartan control the barbarians not only got the power to march or sail wherever they pleased, but they were also established as masters of many Greek cities.

Plataikos 5: Although there was a state of peace and a treaty had been made, we had no share of the general freedom. 17.: (Athens entered the war of 378-374) on behalf of those deprived of freedom in violation of the oaths and the treaties.

Ninth Letter (To Archidamos) 8: These numberless miseries fell chiefly to the lot of those who lived on the coast of Asia whom we gave away not only to barbarians but also to those Greeks who share our language, as the barbarians are wont to do.

Panegyrikos 120-1: Now (the King) is the chief executive of Greek affairs and our commander ... 121: Has he not taken charge of the war, prytanized the Peace and been established as supervisor of current events?

Demosthenes

23.140: Surely it is to our shame that we blame Sparta for having written that the King might do as he wished with the inhabitants of Asia (while we hand people over to Kersebleptes etc.)

15.29: There are two treaties between Greece and the King: one was made by our city and everyone praises it; later the Spartans made the other, the one which everyone reproaches.

Reactions in later writers

Plutarch

Artaxerxes 21.2: The King brought all Greece over to himself at once, so that he arbitrated for the Greeks the notorious Peace which is also known as the Peace of Antalkidas. Antalkidas was a Spartan, son of Leon; through his efforts in the King's interest he convinced the Spartans to concede all the Greek cities in Asia and the neighboring islands as the King's property and subject to his taxes. Thus did the Greeks make peace, if one must so name the rape and betrayal of Greece; no war ever had a more disgraceful conclusion for the losers.

Agesilaus 23.1-2: Sparta decided to make peace with the King. She sent Antalkidas to Tiribazos and most shamefully and immorally betrayed the Greeks in Asia, on whose behalf Agesilaus had fought, to the King ... Antalkidas did this because he was an enemy of Agesilaus, and so spared no effort in obtaining the Peace, apparently because the war brought Agesilaus the highest influence and reputation ... by threats and promises of war, he compelled those who did not desire the Peace to abide by all the conditions laid down by the Persian.

Aristeides

Panathenaicus 172: The Athenians, the last to accede to the Peace, submitted only when they realized that they would have to fight not only the King, Seuthes, Dionysios and the Peloponnesians as well as the Spartans . . . but also their own allies.

Leuctricus 460 and 618: . . . The Spartans besides counting the King as their ally (in the Decelean War) . . . also settled (the Corinthian War) through him, sending Antalkidas to give him the Greeks as the price of peace.

. . . (The Peace) laid it down that the Greeks in Asia belonged to the King to use as he wished.

16. PHANOKRITOS OF PARION IS PUBLICLY HONORED BY ATHENS, 386 B.C.
Tod 116

Parion is on the Asiatic side of the Hellespont. Phanokritos' status in the military action for which he is honored is unknown, but it is difficult not to think that he had observed the movements of Antalkidas' fleet against the Hellespont (see No. 15) and that his information could have greatly altered the course of the war. The situation is very similar to Aegospotami, when Alkibiades' advice was also ignored by the commanding officers (Xenophon, *Hellenica* 2.1.25-6).

[The beginning is lost.]
. . . to give him . . . as reward for his information, if the people agree, and to record his status as benefactor on a stone stele on the Acropolis. Also he is to be invited to dine at the Prytaneion tomorrow. Kephalos moved: let the recommendations of the Council be approved, but let it also be recorded that Phanokritos of Parion is designated as *proxenos* and benefactor, and his descendants as well as himself, on a stone stele, and let the secretary of the Council erect it on the Acropolis, because he reported to the generals that the ships were sailing past. If the generals had acted on the report, the enemy ships would have been captured. Therefore, let him be granted the status of *proxenos* and benefactor and be invited to dine at the Prytaneion tomorrow. Let the *apodektai* set aside the aforesaid money out of the funds on hand after they have budgeted what the law requires.

17. TREATY OF ALLIANCE BETWEEN ATHENS AND CHIOS, 384 B.C.
Tod 118

At the signing of the King's Peace (No. 15) Sparta had insisted that the "autonomy clause" required the separation of Corinth from Argos and the dissolution of Thebes' Boeotian League (see No. 3, XVI). In 385 B.C. Sparta had also insisted that the Peace required the Arcadian city of Mantinea (synoecized ca. 500 B.C.) to dissolve itself back into the five original villages. A seige commanded by the young King Agesipolis (son of King Pausanias; see Nos. 6 and 18) forced the issue, and the new towns were run by pro-Spartan oligarchies. Sparta was now plainly using the "autonomy clause" to implement a policy of "divide and conquer."

Athenian statesmen, eager to use the freedom gained by the Corinthian War without incurring perils based on the "autonomy clause," struck the following alliance with Chios which stresses that it is thoroughly "law-abiding" and in no way violates the King's Peace. This treaty was the first step in the formation of the Second Athenian Confederacy (see Nos. 19-23, 25, 26 and 29-31).

Alliance of Athens and Chios, in the archonship of Dieitrephes (384/3), when Hippothontis held the first prytany (ca. July 384) and ... son of Stephanos from Oion was secretary ... Since the Chians have, like the Athenians, been mindful to guard the written agreements of the Greeks, the peace treaty, the assurances of friendship, the oaths and the existing treaties, which were sworn to by the King, the Athenians, the Lacedaemonians and the other Greeks, and because they have come with good tidings for Athens, all Greece and the King, the assembly has voted as follows: The people of Chios and their ambassadors are to be publicly commended. While upholding the peace treaty, the oaths and the existing treaties, an alliance is to be made with the Chians upon terms of liberty and autonomy. In becoming allies they in no way infringe the peace treaty as it is written upon the stelai, and they would do their best to prevent anyone else from infringing it. A stele is to be erected on the Acropolis in front of the statue of Athena Promachos. It is to be inscribed that, if anyone attacks the Athenians, the Chians will give aid with all possible strength, and if anyone attacks the Chians, the Athenians will give aid with all possible strength. The Council, the generals, and the taxiarchs are to swear the oaths to the Chian ambassadors. In Chios their Council and other magistrates will swear the oaths. Five men are to be selected to sail to Chios and receive the oaths from the Chians. This alliance is without time-limit. The Chian embassy is to be invited to dine in the Prytaneion tomorrow.

The following were selected: Kephalos from Kollytos, ... from Alopeke, Aisimos ... from Phrearrioi, and Demokleides ... The following were the Chian ambassadors: Bryon, Ape ... , ... ritos, and Archelas.

18. PAUSANIAS HONORS HIS SON AGESIPOLIS, 381/0 B.C.
Tod 120

This is a monument erected at Delphi by the Spartan King for his dead son. Pausanias had gone into exile at Tegea as a result of his late arrival during the Haliartos campaign of 395 B.C. (see No. 6). His young son Agesipolis directly succeeded to the throne, and his first activities were in 388/7 B.C. against Argos. He captured Mantinea in 385 B.C. (see No. 17); he died from disease while attacking Olynthos in 380 B.C. The campaign for Olynthos deserves a double digression:

This city was the strongest in the area of the Chalcidice, to the east of Macedon. In 384 B.C. delegates from the other cities in the area complained to Sparta that they were being forced into an alliance with Olynthos to form a Chalcidian League. Sparta considered the growth of Olynthos a threat which could be met as a violation of the King's Peace. In the course of the war on Olynthos (383-379 B.C.) Agesipolis as well as Agesilaus' brother Teleutias died, but Sparta's victory made her supreme in Greece once again (Xenophon, *Hellenica* 5.3.27).

Early in the war against Olynthos, the Spartan Phoibidas, leading an advance expedition northwards in 383 B.C., took the opportunity of attacking and capturing the citadel of Thebes. He installed a pro-Spartan oligarchy supported by a Spartan garrison. Sparta punished Phoibidas lightly and kept control of Thebes. This incident, together with the Sphodrias affair of 378 B.C. when the Spartans tried to capture the Peiraieus (see No. 21), was an indication of how Sparta meant to interpret the terms of the King's Peace. These events led to the war of 378-371 B.C. and Sparta's humiliation in 371 B.C. at Leuctra.

I am a monument which father Pausanias
    set up for his son Agesipolis, whose valor Hellas intones.
        Kleon of Sikyon made me.

19. TREATY OF ALLIANCE BETWEEN ATHENS AND BYZANTIUM, 378/7 B.C.
Tod 121

In the years between the King's Peace and the re-eruption of general war in 377 B.C., Sparta had used her position as self-styled protector of the Peace to gain widespread domination over Greece (see No. 18). Athens, however, was not idle; she allied with Chios in 384 B.C. (No. 17) and with other states afterwards. Eventually Athens reorganized these alliances into a regular confederacy so that the states were allies of each other as well as allies of Athens. The Confederacy was provided with a council called the *synhedrion*, consisting of the allies' representatives in which each city had one vote. Athens herself stood outside the *synhedrion*, and the *synhedrion*'s decision was balanced by that of Athens. In the following inscription Byzantium is added to the *synhedrion*. At this time the only other members were Chios, probably Mytilene, and possibly Rhodes.

Whereas the Byzantines have been steady friends of Athens, both now and in former times, the Assembly voted as follows: Byzantium is to be an ally of Athens and the other allies on the same terms as the Chians. Athens will swear her oaths through the Council, the generals and the hipparchs ... and the Byzantine envoys are to be invited to dine tomorrow in the Prytaneion. The secretary of the Council will have the stele inscribed.

The following were chosen as ambassadors: Orthoboulos from Kerameis, Exekestides from Pallene, Xenodokos from Acharne, Pyrrhandros from Anaphlystos, and Alkimachos from Angele. The following were the Byzantine ambassadors: Kydon, Menestratos, Hegemon, Hestiaios, ... Philinos.

20. TREATY OF ALLIANCE BETWEEN ATHENS AND METHYMNA, 377 B.C.
Tod 122

This inscription shows that Methymna was already allied with Athens; now her alliance is extended to the others as well, and she is added to the *synhedrion*. The procedure for admitting a new member appears slightly more complicated than that in the case of Byzantium (No. 19). The new member must now exchange oaths with the other allies as well as with Athens.

Decree of the Council and Assembly: ... held the prytany, Kall ... from Alopeke was secretary, Simon ... presided, Astyphilos made the motion: Concerning the report of the Methymnaians — whereas the Methymnaians are allies and friends of the Athenian state, in order that the terms of their alliance be the same as for other allies of Athens, the secretary of the Council is to have them inscribed in the same fashion as the other allies of Athens are inscribed. The Methymnaian embassy is to swear the same oath as te other allies swore to the allied representatives (*synhedroi*), the generals and the hipparchs. The *synhedroi* likewise are to swear the same oath to the Methymnaians. Aisimos and the *synhedroi* are to see to it that the magistrates of Methymna swear the same oath as the other allies swore. The city of Methymna is to be publicly commended and her ambassadors invited to dine.

21. THEBES JOINS THE SECOND ATHENIAN CONFEDERACY, 378/7 B.C.
Bengtson 255 = *IG* II^2 40

After Phoibidas captured the citadel of Thebes (see No. 18), Thebes was governed by a pro-Spartan oligarchy. Athens gave refuge to many exiled democrats and patriots. Seven such exiles daringly entered Thebes in the winter of 379/8 B.C., assassinated the chief oligarchs, revived the office of Boeotarch (implying the renewal of the Boeotian League which had been dissolved in 387/6 B.C., No. 17 and No. 3 XVI) and expelled the Spartan garrison. War with Sparta quickly followed. Athens did not openly and firmly take sides, until the affair of the Spartan Sphodrias. This man attempted to capture the Peiraieus in a sneak attack, and Sparta's failure to punish him proved the last straw. Athens came to the aid of Thebes. The initial alliance was soon replaced, as the following document shows, by Thebes' reception into the Confederacy. The "stele of the Allies" mentioned in this inscription must refer to No. 22, in which the Thebans were inscribed at the same time as the rest of that decree. Hence, the two decrees are very close in date.

[The beginning is lost.]
... let the oaths be sworn by seventeen Thebans. Let us invite the Theban ambassadors and ... to dine tomorrow in the Prytaneion. Stephanos moved as follows: concerning the report of

the ambassadors to the allies, let us approve the action of the Council, but also let us add public praise for ... Theopompos, ... and the trierarch Aristomachos, and invite them to dine at the Prytaneion tomorrow. Also let us publicly commend Antimachos of Chios and ... of Mytilene and invite them to dine at the Prytaneion tomorrow. The secretary of the Council will inscribe their names on the stele in accordance with the decree of the Council concerning the treaty on the Stele of the Allies. If there is any conflict with the stele now standing on the Acropolis, let the Council schedule the matter for a vote by the assembly. ... of the Mytilenean, let the Council schedule the matter for a vote by the Assembly. Let the *apodektai* disburse thirty drachmas for the inscribing of each stele, and let the secretary of the Council see to its inscription.

22. THE DECREE OF ARISTOTELES, 377 B.C.
Tod 123

The content and elaborateness of the following document make it the "Queen of Fourth Century Inscriptions." It is sometimes referred to as the "charter" of the Second Athenian Confederacy. This is a misnomer, however, because this decree does not, for example, institute or explain the structure of the *synhedrion*. This body, one of the most distinctive features of the Confederacy, was, as we have seen (No. 19), already in existence. The purpose of this decree is rather to open the Confederacy to the public through a statement of principles. Spartan aggression (see Nos. 18 and 21) is named as the chief target, and the terms of the King's Peace (No. 15) are upheld. The central portion of the decree protects the allies from the most unpopular features of the fifth century empire of Athens. Athens promises not to impose garrisons, tribute or governments on the allies, nor to own land in allied territory. The purpose of the embassy to Thebes is uncertain. The rest of the inscription (apart from some fragments — not translated here — of a rider by Aristoteles) is given to the list of the members, beginning with those who were already allies at the time of this decree, and kept up to date with new additions (and perhaps some deletions) for some years afterwards. For separate records of such accessions, see Nos. 23 (Chalkis) and 25-26 (Corcyra, Akarnania and Kephallenia).

In the archonship of Nausinikos (378/7), Kallibios son of Kephisophon from Paiania was secretary. Hippothontis held the seventh prytany (February/March 377), the Assembly decreed as follows. Charinos from Athmone presided, and Aristoteles made the motion:

May it benefit Athens and her allies — in order that the Spartans may allow the Greeks to have freedom, autonomy, tranquillity and security in the possession of their lands, and in order that the common peace to which Greece and the King of Persia swore by treaty may abide in force forever, the Assembly has voted as follows. If anyone, Greek or otherwise, in Europe or the islands not owned by the King desires to be an ally of Athens and her allies, he may do so and keep his freedom and autonomy. He may have such form of government as please him and will not have imposed upon him any garrison, governor or tribute. The terms of the alliance will be the same as those already existing with Chios, Thebes and the others. For those who make alliance, the Assembly will release any property owned by Athens or by Athenians in the territory of the new ally and give pledges to that effect. If there should exist in Athens any inscription unfavorable to the new ally, the Council has authority to destroy it. After the archonship of Nausinikos it will be illegal for Athens or Athenians to possess land or buildings by purchase or as security or otherwise in allied territory. If anyone does buy or in any way possess such property, any ally may denounce him to the allied *synhedroi*; the *synhedroi* will confiscate the property and give half the proceeds to the accuser, and the rest will be shared among the allies. If anyone makes war upon the allies by land or sea, Athens and the allies will help them with all their might by land and sea. If anyone, magistrate or citizen, should move or put to vote any proposal contrary to this decree or any of its terms, he will lose his citizenship, his property will be confiscated with a tithe going to the Goddess, and he will be tried by Athens and the allies as an enemy of the Confederacy. They will punish him with death or exile from the territory of the Confederacy. If he is executed, he will not be buried in Attica or in allied territory. Let the secretary of the Council have this decree inscribed on a stone stele and erected next to the statue of Zeus the Liberator. Let the treasurers of the Goddess disburse from the Ten Talents sixty drachmas for the inscription on the stele. Let the stele also contain the names of the present allies and of any future allies as well. Let all the foregoing be inscribed, and let the assembly choose immediately three men as envoys to Thebes to persuade the Thebans to whatever good they can. The following were chosen: Aristoteles from Marathon, Pyrrhandros from Anaphlystos and Thrasyboulos from Kollytos. The following are allies of Athens: (at the date of this decree) Chios, Mytilene, Methymna, Rhodes, Byzantium, Thebes; (added shortly afterwards) Chalkis, Eretria, Arethousa, Karystos, Ikos; (added about 377) Perinthos, Peparethos, Skiathos, Maroneia, Dion; (added about 376) Pallene ... Paros, Athenai; (added about 375) the Zakynthians in Nellos, the democracy of Corcyra, Akarnania, Pronnoi in Kephallenia, Alketas, Neoptolemos, Jason (the name Jason is discernible here, but was deleted when he left the Confederacy ca. 371), Abdera, Thasos, the Chalcidians of Thrace, Ainos, Samothrace, Dikaiopolis; (added about 375/4 or 373) Andros, Tenos, Hestiaia, Mykonos, Antissa, Eresos, Astraiousa; on Keos — Ioulis, Karthaia, Koresos; Elaious, Amorgos, Selymbria, Siphnos, Sikinos, the Dians from Thrace, and Neopolis.

23. TREATY OF ALLIANCE BETWEEN CHALKIS AND ATHENS, 377 B.C.
Tod 124

Together with other cities of Euboia, Chalkis joined the Confederacy shortly after the publication of No. 22. She left the Confederacy and allied with Thebes after the Battle of Leuctra in 371 B.C. (see No. 33).

Aristoteles son of Euphiletos from Acharne was secretary. In the archonship of Nausinikos (378/7). A decree of the Council and Assembly. Leontis held the prytany, Aristoteles was secretary, Pantaretos from ..., a *proedros*, put the motion to the vote, Pyrrhandros made the motion. Concerning the report of the Chalcidians: let them be present at the next meeting of the Assembly when it considers the Council's recommendation to accept — with the hope of good fortune — the alliance as offered by the Chalcidians. Let the city swear the oaths to the Chalcidians and the Chalcidians to the Athenians, and let the oaths and the treaty be inscribed on a stone stele and erected in Athens on the Acropolis and in Chalkis in the sanctuary of Athena. The treaty between Athens and Chalkis is as follows: Alliance between Chalkis in Euboia and Athens — Chalkis will keep her own land and be free, autonomous, and ... neither receiving Athenian garrisons, nor paying tribute, nor receiving a governor, as would all be contrary to the decree of the allies. If anyone attacks with warlike intent the land ...

[The end is lost.]

24. ATHENIAN AMPHICTYONS AT DELOS, 377 B.C.
Tod 125, abridged

After the Persian Wars of the fifth century, Athens used the island of Delos as the headquarters for her League until 454/3 B.C.; but throughout the fifth century she held control of the cult of Apollo on Delos and managed the affairs of that sanctuary. Delos was "liberated" by Sparta after the Peloponnesian War, but was retaken by Athens during the Corinthian War (*IG* II^2 1634). Athens may have lost control of Delos after the King's Peace of 387/6 B.C., but in the next decade she was once again in charge and remained so until 314 B.C.

Gods. The following are the transactions of the Athenian Amphictyons, from the archonship (in Athens) of Kalleas (377/6) until Thargelion of the archonship of Hippodamas (ca. May 374) or from the archonship in Delos of Epigenes until Thargelion of the archonship of Hippias. Diodoros son of Olympiodoros from Skambonidai served as secretary to the men who were Amphicytons in this period: (the Amphictyons and their terms of office:) Idiotes son of Theogenes from Acharne — from the archonship of Charisandros (376/5) until Hekatombaion of the archonship of Hippodamas (ca. July 375); Sosigenes son of Sosiades from Xypete — during the archonship of Kalleas (377/6); (the Amphictyons during the entire period) Epigenes son of Metagenes from Koile, Antimachos son of Euthynomos from Marathon and Epikrates son of Menestratos from Pallene.

The following states paid interest:

Mykonos		1260 dr.
Syros		2300 dr.
Tenos	1 talent	
Keos		5472 dr. 4½ ob.
Seriphos		1600 dr.
Siphnos		3190 dr. 4 ob.
Ios		800 dr.
Paros		2970 dr.
Oinaians from Ikaros		4000 dr.
Thermaians from Ikaros		400 dr.
Total of interest paid by states	4 talents	3993 dr. 2½ ob.

The following individuals paid interest:

Ariston of Delos, on behalf of Apollodoros of Delos	900 dr.
Artysileos of Delos, on behalf of Glauketas of Delos	700 dr.
Hypsoklees of Delos	300 dr.
Agasiklees of Delos, on behalf of Theokydes of Delos	630 dr.
Theognetos of Delos, on behalf of Hypsoklees of Delos	312 dr. 3 ob.
Antipatros of Delos, on behalf of Hypsoklees of Delos	287 dr. 3 ob.
Poly... of Tenos, on behalf of M...menes of Tenos	400 dr.
Leukinos of Delos, on behalf of Kleitarchos of Delos	935 dr.
Leophon of Delos, on behalf of Pistoxenos of Delos	350 dr.
Patroklees of Delos, on behalf of Hypsoklees of Delos	300 dr.

Aristeides of Tenos, on behalf of Oiniades of Tenos	210 dr.
Total of interest received from individuals was	5325 dr.
Exacted from the property of Episthenes of Delos as the result of information	380 dr.
Exacted from the property of Python of Delos as the result of information	1100 dr.
Total of fines taken by distraint from losers of lawsuits	1845 dr.
Rents from sanctuaries in Rheneia during the archonships in Athens of Charisandros and Hippodamas, in Delos of Galaios and Hippias	2 talents 1220 dr.
Rents from sanctuaries in Delos during the same period	2484 dr.
Rents of houses during the archonship of Hippodamas in Athens and of Hippias in Delos	297 dr.
Total of all the above receipts	8 talents 4644 dr. 2½ ob.

From this sum the following expenditures were made:

a garland for a perfect victim for the god, materials and labor	1100 dr.
victory tripods for the dancers, materials and labor	1000+ dr.
to the leaders of the sacred embassy	1 talent
transport for the sacred ambassadors and the dancers, paid to the ship's captain Antimachos son of Philon from Hermos	1 talent 1000 dr.

the number of oxen purchased
for the festivals was 109, and
the cost of them was   1 talent   2419 dr.
gold leaf, and the gilder's labor   125+ dr.
for sacrifices before the festival   ...
transport of tripods and oxen,
including 2% customs duty and
food for the oxen and the cost
of timber ...

25. TREATY OF ALLIANCE OF CORCYRA, AKARNANIA AND KEPHALLENIA WITH ATHENS, 375 B.C.
Tod 126

Here we must recapitulate the course of the war which broke out after the liberation of Thebes and the attempt on Peiraieus by Sphodrias in 378 B.C. The fate of Thebes was the main issue in the early stages. Agesilaus invaded Boeotia in the summer of 378 and again in 377 B.C. in order to prevent Thebes from regaining control of Boeotia and hoping even to defeat and recapture Thebes. He ravaged widely in Theban territory and caused her to run short of food, but Theban resistance, aided by Athens, prevented any Spartan gains. Kleombrotos was completely blocked from invading Boeotia in 376 B.C., and Thebes remained free from attack for several years and was able to regain her domination of Boeotia. Stymied on land, Sparta attacked at sea in 376 B.C., attempting to block Athens' food supply with raiders based on Aigina and the Cyclades. Athens countered, and the result of that campaign was a total victory for the Athenian navy in a battle near Naxos. Like Conon's victory at Knidos in 394 B.C., the Battle of Naxos put all subsequent naval operations firmly under Athens' control. After this victory several new allies, some of whom were the states mentioned in the following inscription, joined the Confederacy.

Philokles ... was secretary. In the archonship of Hippodamas (375/4), Antiochis held the second prytany (ca. August 375), when Phylakos from Oinoe was secretary. Decree of the Council and Assembly, Kritios moved: concerning the report of the Corcyrean, Akarnanian, and Kephallenian ambassadors, let us commend the ambassadors of Corcyra, Akarnania, and Kephallenia, because they have been well-disposed towards the people of Athens and the allies, both now and in time past. In order that they may accomplish what they wish, let them be presented to the Assembly together with the Council's recommendation to have its secretary inscribe the names of the states mentioned above onto the Stele of the Allies and to have the Council, generals, and knights swear the oaths to those cities; the allies are also to swear likewise. When this has been done, let the Assembly choose, as it pleases the allies, men to receive the oaths from these cities, who will be inscribed upon the Stele of the Allies. Let each of these cities send *synhedroi* to the allied *synhedrion* in accordance with the decrees of the allies and the Athenian Assembly. Concerning the Akarnanians, let there be a joint inquiry in concert with Aischylos, Euchares, Eury... and Rhysiades.

[The rest is fragmentary.]

26. TREATY OF ALLIANCE BETWEEN ATHENS AND CORCYRA, 375 B.C.
Tod 127

Corcyra joined the Second Athenian Confederacy, as reported in the previous document. The following inscription presents the detailed text for the terms of the alliance and for the oaths to be sworn by the two states.

Alliance without time-limit between Corcyra and Athens. If anyone attacks the land or people of Corcyra with war like intent, the Athenians will give aid with all possible strength, as Corcyra may request. And if anyone attacks Athens or her people with warlike intent by land or sea, Corcyra will give aid with all possible strength, as Athens may request. Corcyra will not make war or peace without the approval of Athens and a majority of the allies; and all other actions will be in accord with the decrees of the allies.

The Oaths

I will aid the people of Corcyra with all possible strength, as they may request, if anyone attacks their land with warlike intent by land or sea, and I will make war and peace in accord with the majority of the allies, as in all other matters. This is true, by Zeus, Apollo and Demeter. May good result if I keep the oath, evil if I do not.

I will aid the people of Athens with all possible strength, as they may request, if anyone attacks their land with warlike intent by land or sea, and I will make war and peace in accord with the Athenians and the majority of the allies, as also in all other matters. This is true, by Zeus, Apollo and Demeter. May good result if I keep the oath, evil if I do not.

27. JASON OF PHERAI
Xenophon, *Hellenica* 6.1.4-16

Athens and Sparta dominate classical Greek history. Other states, to various degrees, lagged behind in political organization and military strength. One of the most important features of the fourth century is the weakening of this domination, as obscure or peripheral states catch up and attain some prominence. The greatest such success was the rise of Macedon (see Nos. 50 and 73), which became the leader of Greece, conquered the East and remained as a world power in Hellenistic times. Another example is the decade of Theban supremacy 371-362 B.C. (see Nos. 33, 34, 36, 42 and 46). Arcadia and Aetolia, strong states in the Hellenistic period, trace their rise from the mid-fourth century (see Nos. 39 and 46), as does Thessaly.

Thessaly was a fertile and populous region, strong in cavalry. Its political organization was quasi-feudal, with a class of serfs and a few large towns run by aristocratic families. The towns acted normally as separate states; at some times, however, these "princedoms" might be united under a single leader (called a *tagos*). The 370s B.C. saw the emergence of such a leader, Jason of Pherai. In his drive to become *tagos*, Jason was opposed by Polydamas of Pharsalos. Jason showed Polydamas that resistance was hopeless unless some outside power intervened; otherwise, the sensible thing was to become allies. Polydamas' unsuccessful appeal to Sparta for help against Jason is presented in the following speech from Xenophon. It offers a gripping analysis of Jason's world-storming character and ambitions. Jason's hopes to unite Thessaly and lead it to total supremacy portend the achievements of Philip of Macedon.

I know that even you Spartans have heard the name of Jason owing to his great power and notoriety. After he and I made a truce, he came to me and said: "Polydamas, I would be able to force your city to join with me, as you may see for yourself from the following considerations. I hold as allies the largest and strongest cities of Thessaly, and I overcame them even while you were aiding them against me. You know, I am sure, that I command six thousand mercenary soldiers, a force which no city could easily contend with, and I can double their number from my other sources. The armies of the cities, by contrast, have soldiers who are past their prime, and many who are not yet mature; and there are few men in any city who actually train their bodies. But I have no soldier in my pay who is not able to match me in every exercise." Jason is in fact — I must be frank with you — an extremely muscular man and fond of physical activity. He tests his company every day by taking the lead, fully-armed, both on the training ground and on campaign. He throws out any mercenaries found to be soft; but he honors those who are energetic and daring in war with double, triple, quadruple pay and with other gifts. He cares for them when they are sick and tends their graves. In this way his hired soldiers know that their martial prowess will bring them a most rich and honored life. He showed me, though I knew it already, that he was master of the Marakoi and the Dolopes and of Alketas, now his lieutenant in Epirus. "How then," he said, "should I fear that I would not easily subdue you? Someone who does not know me might well ask why I wait and do not directly attack Pharsalos. Because, by God, I think it is in every way better to bring you over willingly than otherwise. If I forced you, you would plot against me to the best of your ability, and I would want to keep you as weak as possible. But if you were persuaded to come in with me, then, plainly, we would both benefit. I observe, Polydamas, that the eyes of your country are upon you. If you make it friendly to me, I promise that I will make you the greatest man in Greece, second only to myself. Listen to the projects of which I will give you second command, and don't believe anything I say unless your own calculations prove it to be true. To begin with, we see clearly that, once Pharsalos and its dependencies join me, I will easily be established as *tagos* of all Thessaly. When Thessaly has a *tagos*, its cavalry are six thousand in number and its hoplites more than ten thousand. When I observe the strength and courage of these troops, I think that proper use of them would make Thessaly subject to no other people. The land of Thessaly is a great wide land, and all the neighboring peoples are Thessaly's subjects whenever there is a *tagos*. Most of these tribes fight with the javelin, so that we would have overwhelming strength in light-armed troops. The Boeotians and all the others who are at war with Sparta, are my allies and will follow me once I have freed them from Sparta. I know that Athens would do anything to become our allies, but I do not think I would accept them as friends, because I expect to win command of the sea even more easily than supremacy on land. See if you follow my calculations. Athens gets her ship-timber from Macedon; with Macedon in our power we will be able to outdo Athens in building ships. Who do you think will be better able to provide crews: Athens, or Thessaly with its splendid body of serfs? Which of the two states could feed its sailors better — Thessaly with her abundance of food that she exports to other places, or Athens which cannot feed herself without importing food? Surely we will also have greater abundance of money, drawing our revenues from the nations of the mainland instead of from small islands. The neighboring peoples all pay tribute to Thessaly, whenever there is a *tagos*. You know that the King of Persia is the richest man on earth precisely because he draws his money from a continent and not from the islands. Speaking of him, I also expect that he will be even easier to conquer than the Greeks, because I know that all the people in that part of the world, except for one, are weak from servitude. And I know that he nearly lost everything at the hands of the small forces led by Cyrus and Agesilaus." When he had said all this, I answered that it appeared valid in itself, but that I could not desert Sparta, my ally, and join her opponents when I had no complaints against her. He approved my scruples and said that they made him even more eager to have me as an ally. He released me to come here and report the fact that he means to attack Pharsalos unless I meet his terms. He directed me to ask you for help. "And if," he said, "they let you persuade them to send an army capable of fighting me, then we will await the result of battle. But if you do not think they can send enough help, then no one could blame you for honorably doing what is best for yourself and your city which respects you." Such is the reason for my visit. I am telling you what I myself saw and what I heard from him. My opinion, Spartans, is that if you will send a force large enough to co-operate with me and the other cities of Thessaly against Jason, then the cities will desert him. All are terrified to think how far his power might grow. If, however, you think that freedmen commanded by anyone less than one of your kings will suffice, than I pray you to do nothing at all. You must realize that we would be fighting a mighty strength and a man who is a canny general. He makes few mistakes, whether in acting in stealth, striking the first blow or using open force. He works by night as well as by day. When he is in haste he eats while he works. He rests only when he has arrived at his destination and finished the campaign; and he has trained all his men to be just like him. When his men push themselves to victory, he knows exactly how to satisfy their expectations for rewards. All of his men have learned that hard work brings luxury. He is the most self-controlled man I know of. Desire for pleasure never causes him to ignore duty. Therefore, consider the problem and tell me, as you ought, what you can and will do about it.

28. THE PEACE OF 375/4 B.C.
Bengtson 265

In answer to Polydamas, Sparta regretfully decided that her forces were already overextended. In the war with Thebes and Athens Sparta had been driven from the seas (see No. 25), and land operations were also not going well. Sparta was thus receptive to a peace movement which came at this time. The treaty was a "common peace" which was essentially a renewal of the King's Peace (see No. 15). In the section below Diodorus is probably correct about the involvement of Persia, but wrong about the exclusion of Thebes from the peace. He has most likely confused this peace with that of 371 B.C. (see No. 34). Xenophon's presentation of Athenian motives may be correct as far as it goes. The peace, however, certainly represented a victory for the Athenian Confederacy and the goals announced in 377 B.C. (see No. 22).

Athens received the settlement with joy as seen in C and D and in Kephisodotos' publicly commissioned statue of Peace and her offspring

Wealth (Plate p. 51). The bases of the statues for Timotheos and his father Conon (see No. 3) also survive (Tod 128).

The peace lasted only a short time; in the course of terminating his campaign the Athenian general Timotheos returned some exiled democrats to Zakynthos (listed in No. 22). The Spartans denounced this act as a violation of Zakynthian autonomy, and newly allied with Dionysios of Syracuse they rushed back into war.

A. Xenophon, *Hellenica* 6.2.1: The Athenians, seeing that they were causing Thebes to grow strong, while Thebes contributed nothing to the fleet and Athens was being worn down by the capital levies, the piracy from Aigina, and the consequent posting of guards on Attica, decided to end the war. They sent envoys to Sparta and made peace.

B. Diodorus Siculus 15.38.1-4: Artaxerxes the Persian King, intending to attack Egypt and anxious to collect a decent mercenary force, decided to end the state of war in Greece. He thought that Greeks would be especially ready to enlist with him once their wars at home were stopped. He therefore sent envoys to Greece summoning the cities to make a common peace. The Greeks, tired of the continuous warfare, accepted his proposals with pleasure. Everyone made peace on terms of leaving the cities autonomous and ungarrisoned. The Greeks appointed officials who went to each city and removed the garrisons. The Thebans alone refused to let the peace be made by individual cities, because they counted all Boeotia as subject to Thebes. The Athenians opposed them most zealously through the oratory of the politician Kallistratos. In the *synhedrion* Epameinondas spoke admirably on behalf of Thebes. Thus the treaty was made with the approval of all Greece except for the Thebans who were declared outcasts from it. The courage of Epameinondas filled the Thebans with the hope of resisting the common decrees. Sparta and Athens, always constant rivals for hegemony, deferred to each other so that one should rule the land, the other the sea.

C. Nepos, *Timotheus* 2.3: Thereupon the Spartans ceased the long struggle and of their own initiative conceded naval supremacy to Athens, making peace on terms of Athenian command of the sea. This success was such a cause of joy to the Athenians that for

Plate III Eirene (Peace) and the infant Ploutos (Wealth), 375/4 B.C. (Courtesy of the Antikensammlung, Munich)

the first time an altar of Peace was built by the state and a *pulvinar* was established for the goddess. A statue of Timotheos was publicly erected in the city square to preserve his memory.

D. Isocrates, *Antidosis* 109-110: Timotheos also forced the Spartans to make this Peace which worked such a change for each city. Since that day we give annual sacrifice to Peace, because it was uniquely beneficial to our city.

29. TREATY OF ALLIANCE BETWEEN AMYNTAS AND ATHENS, 375-373 B.C.
Tod 129

In order to counterbalance the hostile Chalcidian League (see No. 12), Amyntas turned to Sparta sometime after 390 B.C. When Sparta forced Olynthos to join her own League in 379 B.C. and began also interfering in Macedonian affairs, Amyntas about 375 turned to Athens. He probably joined the Second Athenian Confederacy and recognized Athens' claims to Amphipolis as Amphipolis' mother city. Athens had colonized Amphipolis in 437 B.C., but the Athenians remained a minority, while other peoples, Chalcidians and eastern Greeks, also settled in the city which controlled the Strymon valley with its timber and gold mines. In 424 B.C. Brasidas, the Spartan general, had won over Amphipolis, and, although the Peace of Nikias in 421 required Amphipolis to be returned to Athens, she remained independent until captured by Philip (see No. 50).

Although Amyntas was unable to render effective military aid to Athens, he did have ship timber to offer the Athenians for their help against the Spartans and the Chalcidian League. Macedon's timber made her a highly desirable ally (see Meiggs-Lewis 91 = Tod 91; Nos. 12 and 27).

[The beginning is lost.]
... men (were elected) to administer the oath to Amyntas and Alexander (son of Amyntas) and to see to the publication of the decree so that the decrees of the people may become effective. The Athenians commend Amyntas and his envoys, Ptolemy, Antenor and ... who came to Athens. The Athenians also commend their own envoys whom the people sent to Macedon to negotiate the alliance. The Treasurer of the People is to give each

of the newly elected envoys twenty drachmas for travel expenses. Let the ambassadors of Amyntas and also the Athenian envoys be invited to dine at the Prytaneion tomorrow.

30. ATHENIAN NAVY RECORDS, ca. 372 B.C.
IG II^2 1609, lines 83-110

Athens' infantry were excellent, but her distinctive strength was in naval power. Rich citizens were periodically drafted to supervise the operation of a trireme, a service called the trierarchy. The trierarch was required to operate and maintain his assigned trireme for one year and return it in good condition. The city paid for the crew, but the trierarch had to pay for upkeep of the ship itself. The city also furnished equipment such as oars and rigging, although some trierarchs preferred to furnish their own. The delivery and return of triremes and equipment were supervised by the officials in charge of the dockyards, and these transactions were recorded in stone, as in the following excerpt. Each item gives the name of the ship, the name of its trierarch or trierarchs, and the equipment which he must return to the public stores. These inscriptions are extremely valuable in providing information on the detailed management of Athens' navy. They also frequently allude to matters mentioned elsewhere in the historical sources. The selection below, for example, mentions Apollodoros from Acharne, who is well known as the son of the wealthy freedman Pasion; his trierarchy of 362/1 is the subject of Demosthenes' oration *Against Polykles* (no. 50 in the Demosthenic corpus, generally agreed to be not by Demosthenes and sometimes thought to be by Apollodoros himself). There is also mentioned a cleruchy (cf. Nos. 41 and 48), such as the Athenians had promised (No. 22) not to create in allied territory; the destination of this one is unknown. The names of the triremes are all feminine.

... The *Soizousa* (*Preserver*): her trierarchs are Apollodoros from Acharne and Timokrates from Krioa; they have a complete set of wooden gear which Archestratos from Alopeke contributed; of rigging, they have a sail contributed by Stephanos from Euonymon, white side-shields (to protect the rowers), two anchors contributed by Apollodoros from Acharne, a woven-hair side-shield, an underlay, a tarpaulin (for a shield) which Phil ... from Acharne returned, and cables returned by Pasion from Acharne. During our term of office, this ship was ...

The following triremes went out to found a cleruchy under the leadership of Euktemon from Lousia and Euthios from Sounion. The *Doris* (*Dorian Girl*): her trierarchs are Apollodoros from Acharne and Timokrates from Krioa; she has the following wooden gear: two ladders, two poles, and two mast-props. The *Hegemonia* (*Hegemony*): her trierarchs are Philinos from Lamptrai and Demomeles from Paiania; they took no equipment during our term of office. The *Mousike* (*Finearts*): her trierarchs are Phanostratos from Kephisia and Dorotheos from Eleusis; they took no equipment during our term of office. The *Nike* (*Victory*): she is a new ship built by Pistokrates, and her trierarchs are Deinias from Erchia and Leochares from Pallene; they have taken no equipment during our term of office. The *Hegemonia* (*Hegemony*): she is a new ship built by Lysikrates, and her trierarch is Chabrias from Aixone; he has two hundred oars, and he must return a complete set of oars. The *Eudoxia* (*Glory*): her trierarch is Kallippos from Aixone; he has complete sets of both rigging and wooden gear; this ship was given to the tithe-farmers. The *Bakche* (*Bacchante*): she is a new ship built by Hierophon; her trierarch is Aristaichmos from Cholleidai; he has a complete set of rigging; of wooden gear he has two hundred oars, and he must return a complete set of oars; he also has a large mast. The *Naukratis* (*Naucratis*, an old Greek colony in Egypt, the name also connoting *Seamistress*): she is a new ship built by Xenokles; her trierarchs are Timotheos from Anaphlystos and Theoxenos from Euonymon; of rigging they have a sail, an underlay, a tarpaulin, lines, and anchor-cable; of wooden gear they have two hundred oars, and they must return a complete set of oars. The *Eudia* (*Fairweather*): she is a new ship built by Aristokles; her trierarchs are Charikleides from Myrrhinous (or Myrrhinoutta) and Kallistratos from Aphidna; they have complete sets of both rigging and wooden gear, except for a boat-sail and that they took two hundred oars instead of a complete set of oars; they must, however, return a complete set of oars. The *Amemptos* (*Flawless*): her trierarchs are Philippos from Kolonos and Polykles from Anagyrous; they have a complete set of rigging; of wooden gear they have a large mast, large sails, ladders, and two hundred oars, for which they must return a complete set of oars. They have returned the rigging except for cables and undergirdles, and they have returned a complete set of oars. The *Rhodonia* (*Rhodian*, or

Rosy): her trierarchs are Kleotimides from Atene and Kephalion from Aphidna; they have a complete set of rigging; of wooden gear they have large sails and ladders.

31. DECREES RELATING TO THE SECOND ATHENIAN CONFEDERACY, 372 B.C.
S. Accame, *La lega ateniese del sec. IV a.C.* Rome, 1941, p. 230

The following inscription contains the end of an Athenian decree and the beginning of a decree of the allied *synhedrion*. The Athenian decree was perhaps the consequence of disturbances on Paros similar to the later troubles on Keos (Nos. 44 and 56). Part of the settlement in this case required the Parians to appear with gifts at the chief Athenian festivals as a sign of loyalty. Such duties had been common for the subjects of the fifth century Athenian empire.

The allied decree, it is felt, also concerns the troubles on Paros. The assembly and council mentioned would be the Parian ones, and the "ancient laws" (concerning homicide) would be those of Paros. The decree apparently attempts to assure that complaints arising from the disturbances would be handled legally.

[The beginning is lost]

... in accordance with tradition, and to present at the Panathenaian festival an ox and a panoply, and at the Dionysia an ox and phallos of excellence, since they are colonists of the Athenian people. Let this decree be inscribed, as well as the settlement which the allies made with the Parians, and let it be erected on the Acropolis. Let the Treasurer of the People disburse twenty drachmas for inscribing the stele, and let the Parian ambassadors be invited to dine in the Prytaneion tomorrow.

In the archonship of Asteios (373/2), on the last day of Skirophorion (ca. late June 372), the matter was put to a vote by ... of Thebes, and the allies passed the following decree: Let no one be expelled from house or land, or any violence be done contrary to this decree. If anyone slays, let the council and the assembly condemn the killers to death in accordance with the ancient laws. If anyone expels or banishes another in violation of this decree, let him be disfranchised ...

[The end is lost.]

32. FIRST PEACE TREATY OF 371 B.C.
Bengtson 269

The war that re-erupted in 374 B.C. (No. 28) centered on Corcyra, where Athens helped foil Spartan attacks. Thebes made use of the interval to extend her power in Boeotia and attack her neighbor Phokis. Although Athens had favored the liberation of Thebes in 378 B.C., and although she had Thebes as a member of her Confederacy, she did not wish her northern neighbor to become too strong. Because the Boeotian situation was unsatisfactory (Xenophon, *Hellenica* 6.3.1-2; cf. No. 28), and because the military situation was stalemated, Athens initiated peace-moves. A peace conference held in Sparta produced another Common Peace (see Nos. 15, 28, 34, 47, 67, and 74). Xenophon's presentation of the Athenian speeches (*Hellenica* 6.3.4-17), not translated here, is extremely interesting: it indicates that Sparta, after a thirty-year struggle for control of Greek affairs, was apparently reconciled to the rest of Greece, and that Athens and Sparta rediscovered how to cooperate. Selections A and B below give the terms of the Peace and describe the emergence of Thebes, who wished recognition of her control of Boeotia, as an obstacle to the settlement. Selection B is probably wrong concerning the involvement of Persia, but it is right about the exclusion of Thebes (see No. 28).

A

Xenophon, *Hellenica* 6.3.18-6.4.3: These speeches found favor, and the Spartans as well voted to accept the Peace, on terms of withdrawing their harmosts from the cities, disbanding armaments both naval and military, and leaving the cities autonomous. If the conditions were violated, help could be given to the injured party on a voluntary basis, but no one was required by the treaty to give such help. The Spartans swore to these terms on behalf of themselves and their allies, while Athens and her allies swore separately, city by city. Thebes was also recorded among the cities who took the oath; on the next day, however, the Theban envoys appeared and directed that the record be altered to say that "Boeotia" had sworn, rather than "Thebes." Agesilaus answered that he would not alter a single word in the original record of the oaths; but if they did not wish to share in the treaty, he would comply with a request to erase them. In this way everyone else made peace, but Thebes remained as an object of dispute; and the Athenians expected that the old pledge to destroy Thebes and dedicate a tithe was about to be fulfilled. The Thebans went home in a state of utter despair. Athens then withdrew her garrisons from the cities and sent for Iphicrates and the fleet; everything which he had captured after the oaths were sworn at Sparta had to be given back. Sparta withdrew her harmosts and garrisons from the other cities, but the Spartan authorities debated what should be done with Kleombrotos and his army in Phokis. Prothoos said that he thought they ought to disband the army, as the oaths required, and, next, send round to the cities to voluntarily deposit money in the temple of Apollo; finally, if anybody were violating any state's autonomy, they should summon the supporters of autonomy to march against its opponents. In this way, he said, the gods would be on their side, and the other cities could not complain. When the assembly heard this, they thought he was just drivelling; heaven, apparently, was leading them on to destruction.

B

Diodorus 15.50.4: King Artaxerxes, seeing that Greece was once again in turmoil, sent envoys and summoned the Greeks to end their internal warfare by making a Common Peace according to the previous agreements. All Greece gladly accepted his proposals, and all the cities made a Common Peace, except for Thebes. Thebes alone was excluded from the Peace because she was holding Boeotia in subjection, whereas it had been decided to make the Peace on the basis of separate cities. Outcast from the Peace, just as before, Thebes continued to control Boeotia.

C

Plutarch, *Agesilaus* 28.5: On the 14th of Skirophorion (ca. early June, 371) they made the Peace; they were defeated at Leuktra on the 5th of Hekatombaion (ca. late June, 371), twenty days later.

33. THE BATTLE OF LEUCTRA, 371 B.C.
Tod 130

Thebes had faced a similar situation in 387/6 B.C. (No. 15): at that time she had capitulated, allowed her Boeotian league to be dissolved, and eventually suffered occupation and revolution (No. 18). Now, deserted by Athens, she determined to resist. The Spartan King Kleombrotos succeeded in foiling the defenses of Boeotia's borders and penetrated near to Thebes. The army of Thebes, commanded by the great Epameinondas, intercepted Kleombrotos' march at Leuctra. In the battle, Kleombrotos was killed and his army was disastrously defeated: 400 Spartans, out of 700 engaged, died. Greece was shocked by this humiliation of supposedly invincible Sparta. The following inscription contains three Thebans' memorial of the battle.

>   Xenokrates, Theopompos, Mnasilaos.
>
> When Sparta's spear was strong, then chose
>   Xenokrates a trophy to Zeus Allotter to raise,
> Never fearing Eurotas' army nor Laconia's
>   shield. "The Thebans are stronger in war"
> proclaims that Leuctra-trophy, victory-bearing in our spear,
>   and in the race for glory we were Epameinondas' peer.

34. SECOND PEACE TREATY OF 371 B.C.
Bengtson 270 = Xenophon, *Hellenica* 6.5.1

Athens was displeased with the news from Leuctra, which threatened to upset the desirable situation (cooperation with Sparta on the basis of the King's Peace) established by the treaty. Athens therefore quickly convened another peace conference, at which nearly all states swore their continued support of the Common Peace; note, however, that assistance to threatened states was now made compulsory.

When Archidamos had led the army back from the Leuctra campaign, the Athenians calculated that the Peloponnesians still felt obliged to follow Sparta, and that Sparta was not as yet in the same sort of position as she had put Athens in (i.e. in 404 B.C.). Athens therefore sent to the cities, inviting them to take part in the Peace sent down by the King. When they had assembled, a decree was passed with an oath for those who wished to participate: "I will abide by the treaty sent down by the King, and by the decrees of the Athenians and their allies (i.e., the principles of, e.g., No. 22). If anyone attacks any city which is a party to this oath, I will give aid in all strength." The other cities were pleased with the oath, but Elis objected to recognizing the autonomy of Marganon, Skillous, and Triphylia, claiming these cities as Elian property. The Athenians and the others who voted that all cities, great and small alike, should be autonomous just as the King had written, sent out oath-givers and directed the chief magistrates in each city to take the oath; and all but Elis did so.

35. BOEOTIA HONORS THE CARTHAGINIAN NOBAS, BETWEEN 370 AND 366 B.C.
IG VII 2407 = SIG^3 179

After the Battle of Leuctra in 371 B.C. Thebes was the strongest military power in Greece. As an indication of her new power, she entered into new relations with other Greek states (see Nos. 36 and 42). In this inscription she publicly honors a Carthaginian and makes him her *proxenos*. It has been suggested that Thebes was thinking of building a navy and that the Nobas mentioned in the inscription was a Carthaginian naval adviser (see Thomes, *Egemonia Beotica*, Turin, 1952, pp. 24-30). For the Boeotarchs see No. 3, XVI.

God and Good Fortune. Dioteles was archon. Decree of the people to designate Nobas son of Axioubos of Carthage as *proxenos* and benefactor of the Boeotians, and to grant him the right to own house and land, immunity from our taxes, and inviolability by land and by sea, in war and in peace. Boeotarchs: Timon, Aitondas, Thion, Menon, Hippias, Eumaridas, Patron.

36. THESSALY COMMEMORATES PELOPIDAS, 370-360 B.C.
Wiener Jahreshefte XXXIII, 1941, p. 38

Jason (No. 27) was assassinated in 370 B.C. His nephew Alexander of Pherae attempted to succeed him as *tagos*. Tradition portrays Alexander as a cruel and bloodthirsty tyrant. The other cities were firm in their opposition to his plans to rule all of Thessaly, and they found outside assistance. Alexander II of Macedon brought them support in 369 B.C. More lasting help was brought in 368 B.C. by the Theban Pelopidas, who campaigned successfully and created the Thessalian League to oppose the *tageia* which Alexander was attempting to acquire. This League and its officers are parties to the alliance with Athens in No. 49. During a second expedition Pelopidas was captured by Alexander and was rescued by Epameinondas. Alexander's continued attacks on the League cities led to the decisive intervention of 364 B.C., when Pelopidas defeated Alexander's army at Kynoskephalai. Pelopidas was killed in this battle, but Pherai was forced to become an ally of Thebes, and Thessaly was safe from Alexander until Thebes was weakened by the death of Epameinondas in 362 B.C. The following inscription came from a statue of Pelopidas erected at Delphi by the Thessalians. The sculptor was the famous Lysippos.

> Destroyer of Sparta, who came to our aid,
> with praise, trust, and statue we crown thee.
> Hereafter be it thine more trophies oft
> to raise, Boeotia's leader, glorious one!

The Thessalians dedicated to Pythian Apollo this statue of Pelopidas, son of Hippokles of Thebes. Lysippos son of Lys . . . of Sikyon made it.

37. ATHENS HONORS THE SPARTAN KOROIBOS, 367 B.C.
Tod 135

Athens after the Battle of Leuctra in 371 B.C. feared Thebes (see No. 34). In this inscription Athens honors an otherwise unknown Spartan, Koroibos, and makes him her *proxenos*. The purpose of the embassy to Sparta is also unknown. It seems certain, however, that both the embassy to Sparta and the public praise for Koroibos are signs of the good relations between Athens and Sparta. Thebes had, after the Battle of Leuctra, invaded the Peloponnese, attacked Sparta, and, most importantly, liberated Messenia, ending three and a half centuries of the Spartan enslavement of the Messenians. In 369 B.C. Sparta had allied with Athens to counterbalance Thebes, now the foremost power in Greece. At the same time as this decree honoring Koroibos of Sparta, Athens also allied with Dionysios of Syracuse, a longtime ally of the Spartans (see No. 38).

In the archonship of Nausigenes (368/7), when Aiantis held the seventh prytany (ca. February 367) and Moschos son of Thestios from Kydathenaion was secretary, the Council and Assembly decreed: Aiantis held the prytany, Paramythos from Otryne presided, Moschos son of Thestios from Kydathenaion was secretary, and Diophantos made the motion: concerning the report of the ambassadors from Sparta, the Council has voted that the current *proedroi* all negotiate the matter in the Assembly and present to the Assembly the Council's resolution. The resolution is as follows: whereas Koroibos of Sparta has done good things for the people of Athens, both now and previously, let him — and his descendants as well — be designated as *proxenos* and benefactor of the people of Athens. Let the secretary of the Council inscribe this decree on a stone stele and erect it on the Acropolis; let the Treasurer of the People pay twenty drachmas for the inscribing, from the money which the people have budgeted for decrees.

38. TREATY OF ALLIANCE BETWEEN ATHENS AND DIONYSIOS, 367 B.C.
Tod 136

The Battle of Leuctra (No. 33) and the subsequent activities of Thebes (see Nos. 35, 36, 37, 42) had brought Athens and Sparta closer together. Athens could also now draw closer to Sparta's longtime ally, Dionysios of Syracuse (see No. 11). During the second invasion of the Peloponnese by Epameinondas, Dionysios had sent aid to Athens and Sparta, and in 368 B.C. Athens decreed lavish honors for him (Tod 133). In the next year a formal alliance was made, as shown in the following inscription. Dionysios died shortly afterwards and was succeeded by his son (see No. 76).

In the archonship of Nausigenes (368/7), when Aiantis was holding the seventh prytany (ca. April 367), Moschos from Kydatheniaion was the secretary, on the thirty-second day of the prytany, and the proedros ... son of Daïppos from Marathon put the motion to the vote. The Assembly approved the motion of Pandios: With good luck for Athens, let the people vote to publicly commend Dionysios the governor of Syracuse because he does good to the people of Athens and to the allies. He and his descendants will be allies, without time-limit, of the people of Athens, on the following terms. If anyone attacks in war the land of Athens by sea or by land, Dionysios and his descendants will bring help as the Athenians may request by land and by sea with all his strength as far as possible. And if anyone attacks in war by land or by sea Dionysios or his descendants or anyone whom Dionysios rules, the Athenians will bring aid as requested by land and by sea with all their strength as far as possible. Neither Dionysios nor his descendants may bear arms to harm the land of Athens by land or by sea. And the Athenians may not bear arms to harm Dionysios or his descendants or anyone whom he rules, either by land or by sea. The oaths of the alliance will be received by the ambassadors who have come from Dionysios and be sworn by the Council, the generals, the hipparchs, and the taxiarchs. The oaths will be sworn by Dionysios and the Syracusan archons, council, generals, and trierarchs. Everyone will swear his traditional oath; the oaths will be received by the Athenian ambassadors who sail to Sicily. Let the secretary of the Council have the decree inscribed on a stone stele and erected on the Acropolis. Let the Treasurer of the People give thirty drachmas for inscribing it.

39. ATHENIAN COMPLAINT AGAINST AETOLIA, 367 B.C.
Tod 137

The historical importance of this inscription lies in its mention of the Aetolian League; it is our earliest indication of the existence of this League, which went on to be an important state in Hellenistic history. Aetolia was at this time one of the more backward parts of Greece. Its organization into a League may reflect Theban influence and interest in the area.

Gods. Demophilos son of Theoros from Kephale was the secretary. The Council and Assembly passed the following decree. Oineis held the prytany. Demophilos son of Theoros from Kephale was the secretary; Philippos from Semachidai presided; Polyzelos was archon, and Kephisodotos made the motion: At a time when the Aetolian League had accepted the truce of the Mysteries of Demeter of Eleusis and of Kore, two men, Prophetes and

Epigenes, from the (Athenian clans) Eumolpidai and Kerykes, ambassadors for the truce, were arrested by the city of Trichoneion in violation of all the common laws of the Greeks. The Council recommended the election of a herald from all the Athenians, who will go to the Aetolian League and demand that these men be freed and . . .

40. PLOTS AGAINST MAUSSOLLOS, 367-354 B.C.
Tod 138

Maussollos was the satrap of Caria, ruling as governor for the king of Persia. Maussollos was almost completely independent, allying himself with Greek states and carving out for himself an area of influence in the Aegean (see No. 54). The following inscription records three separate occasions when plots, involving citizens of the Carian city Mylasa, were organized against the life of Maussollos. The first two plots occurred during the reign of Artaxerxes II Mnemon (367/6 and 361/0 B.C.) and the third during the reign of Artaxerxes III Ochos (355/4 B.C.). Mylasa, although subject to Maussollos and the King, still had a civic government.

In the thirty-ninth year of the reign of Artaxerxes (367/6), when Maussollos was satrap, there was a regular assembly of the people with the ratification of the three tribes, and the citizens of Mylasa passed the following decree: When Arlissis son of Oussollos, sent as ambassador by the Carians to the King, played the people false and plotted against Maussollos himself, a benefactor of the city of Mylasa as were also his father Hekatomnos and his ancestors, the King convicted Arlissis of wrongdoing and executed him. The city of Mylasa confiscated Arlissis' property in accordance with the ancestral laws of the city and made it over to Maussollos. The city also invoked curses on anyone who might make a proposal or put a motion up for vote on the way this matter was handled. If anyone violates these rulings, may he and all his children be utterly destroyed.

In the forty-fifth year of the reign of Artaxerxes (361/0), when Maussollos was satrap, there was a regular assembly of the people with the ratification of the three tribes, and the citizens of Mylasa passed the following decree: The sons of Peldemos desecrated the statue of Hekatomnos, a man who had been a benefactor in word and deed to the city of Mylasa; they committed a grave crime against the holy images, the city, and the city's benefactors. Convicted of this crime, they were punished with the confiscation of their property and the public sale of their goods, with the purchasers to have full ownership. The city also invoked curses on anyone who might make a proposal or put a motion up for vote on the way this matter was handled. If anyone violates these rulings, may he and all his children be utterly destroyed.

In the fifth year of the reign of Artaxerxes (355/4), when Maussollos was satrap, Manitas the son of Paktyes plotted against Maussollos the son of Hekatomnos in the sanctuary of Zeus Lambraundos during the annual sacrifices and festival. Maussollos was saved by Zeus and Manitas was punished on the spot, killed in accordance with the law. The citizens of Mylasa determined that Manitas had committed an outrage on the sanctuary and on its benefactor Maussollos. The citizens made an inquiry to see if anyone else took part or was associated in the plot. Thyssos son of Syskos was examined and judged to have been an accomplice of Manitas. The citizens of Mylasa, with the ratification of the three tribes, passed the following decree: The property of Manitas son of Paktyes and the property of Thyssos son of Syskos should be given to Maussollos. The city confiscated and sold their goods, with the purchasers to have full ownership. The city also invoked curses on anyone who might make a proposal or put a motion up for vote on the way this matter was handled. If anyone violates these rulings, may he and all his children be utterly destroyed.

41. ATHENIANS IN SAMOS, 365-324 B.C.
Athenische Mitteilungen LI, 1926, p. 36.

At the beginning of this century the relations between Athens and Samos were extremely warm and generous (No. 1). Our knowledge of their subsequent relations is very obscure, and it is surprising to find that Athens captured Samos in about 365 B.C., drove many Samians from their property, and settled Athenians in their place (Diodoros 18.18.9). The contents of the following inscription prove that Athenians were in residence on Samos. For other Athenian settlements abroad in this period see Nos. 30 and 48.

Gods. ... from Kydathenaion made the following motion: whereas those who (borrowed) money are not paying the interest, with the result that Pandion and the other gods are not receiving sacrifice and the welfare of the tribe is being injured, let them pay back the money, both the principal and the interest, within the year after the archonship of ...atos. If they do not pay back the principal and the interest within that time, let the supervisors of the tribe record them as disfranchised. Let this decree be inscribed on a stone stele and erected on ...

42. BOEOTIA HONORS A BYZANTINE, CA. 365-363 B.C.
IG VII 2408

Byzantium had joined the Second Athenian Confederacy in 378 B.C. (No. 19). Thebes employed the years after Leuktra (No. 33) to widely extend her power and influence (see Nos. 35 and 36). In 365/4 B.C. Epameinondas decided to challenge Athens on the seas. A Boeotian fleet, launched in 364 B.C., cruised in the north Aegean as far as Byzantium. Many allies were detached from the Confederacy of Athens, including Byzantium. The following inscription probably relates to these maneuvers. Epameinondas' naval projects were interrupted by strife in Arcadia, which led to his fourth and final invasion of the Peloponnese, and to the battle of Mantineia (No. 46). Byzantium was soon back in the Confederacy, but later took part in the great secession of 357-355 B.C. (No. 54). Athens and Byzantium allied once again to resist Philip in 340/39 B.C. Byzantium, with the rest of Greece, became subject to Philip after 338 B.C. (No. 74).

... it was decreed by the people ... son of ... of Byzantium shall be designated as *proxenos* and benefactor of the Boeotians, and he shall be granted freedom from taxes, protection, and inviolability during peace or war, by both land and sea. He shall also be granted the right to own house and land. These benefits extend to his descendants as well as to himself. Boeotarchs: Asopodoros, Malekidas, Diogiton, Mixias, Aminadas, Hippias, Aitondas.

43. CONTRIBUTIONS FOR REBUILDING THE TEMPLE AT DELPHI, 363 B.C.
Tod 140

In the winter of 373/2 B.C. the temple of Apollo at Delphi was destroyed by some natural disaster. Soon afterwards an attempt was made to collect funds from all of Greece to rebuild this sacred shrine. The fund-raising drive started in spring 369 B.C. Contributions came from both cities and individuals. The following inscription is from the record of the thirteenth semi-annual drive, that of spring 363 B.C. The money is given in Aeginetan standards; when money of a different standard (such as the Attic) or a gift in kind is given, it is converted to the Aeginetan equivalent. All gifts were recorded, regardless of their size or of the status of the giver.

In the archonship of Aischylos (at Delphi), during the spring term, the thirteenth in the fund-raising drive, the following cities made second contributions:

Megara (Andron was the envoy)	3,444 dr.
Troizen (Phegon was the envoy)	334 dr.
Kypharrha (Kombos was the envoy)	170 dr.

The following cities and individuals made first contributions in the same session:

Naxos (Telesikrates son of Timokleides, and Aristodemos son of Aisimos were the envoys)	350 dr.
Strombon of Naxos	2 dr.
Demainetos of Naxos	10 Attic dr. = 7 Aeginetan dr.
Telesikrates of Naxos	2 dr.
Aristodemos of Naxos	2 dr.
Messenia (Lysixenos, Phillis, ... and Eurybios were the envoys)	70 dr.
Sosibios of Pharsalos	1 dr.
Andokos of Sparta	2 dr.
Lygdamis of Tragila	6 dr., 4 ob.
Naukratis in Egypt (Pythagoras was the envoy)	350 dr.
Eudamos of Syracuse	30 dr.
Saraukos of Arcadia	2 dr.
Kottabos of Arcadia	3 dr.
Eurydika of Larisa	2 dr.

Aischylos of Selinous			2 dr.
Epicharmos of Arcadia			1 dr.
Kleino of Phleious			3 ob.
Echenike of Phleious			1 ½ ob.
Kleonika of Phleious			1 ½ ob.
Philostratis of Sparta			3 ob.
Kleogenes of Athens	4 Attic dr.	=	2 dr., 4 ob. (Aeginetan)
Peisios of Athens	4 Attic dr.	=	2 dr., 4 ob. (Aeginetan)
Kteson of Athens	4 Attic dr.	=	2 dr., 4 ob. (Aeginetan)
Theodoros of Athens, the actor			70 dr.
Euteles			2 dr.
Hegemon			3 ob.
Damothemis Euphaneus of Phaselis			7 dr.
Ariston			1 dr.
Pankon of Thebes			1 dr.
Timeas of Apollonia			70 dr.
Thrasyboulos of Thespiai			1 dr.
Apollonia 3,000 Pheidonian measures of wheat, which equals 1,875 Delphian bushels, which are worth			3,587 dr., 3 ½ ob.
The citizens of Apollonia paid the expense of transporting the wheat across the sea to Delphi. Ainesidemos of Delphi and Aristokleides of Apollonia brought the wheat to Delphi.			

The total contributed during the archonship of Aischylos was   8,530 dr., 1 ½ ob.

44. REBELLIONS IN IOULIS, 362 B.C.
Tod 142

During this period Athens had a great deal of trouble with her allies on the island of Keos. The four cities there revolted; after this revolt was put down, the city of Ioulis rose again in unsuccessful rebellion. The following inscription records the second settlement in Ioulis. During the first revolt, citizens who remaind loyal to Athens had been exiled; they were restored in the first settlement and exiled once again in the second revolt. Restored once again, they discovered that their city owed money to Athens. In the following inscription Athens makes provisions for the repayment of that money, for readministering the oaths of the alliance, for the punishment of those who rebelled the second time, and for the future peace of the city. The final section records the oaths of the Athenians and their allies, of the citizens of Ioulis who did not openly side with either party, and of the citizens of Ioulis who remained loyal to Athens. For further relations between Athens and Keos see Nos. 52 and 61.

Gods. In the archonship of Charikleides (363/2). Aiantis held the prytany, Nikostratos from Pallene was the secretary, and Philittios from Boutadai presided. The Council and Assembly passed the following decree; Aristophon made the motion: Since those citizens of Ioulis whom the Athenians restored say that the city of Ioulis owes Athens three talents of the money calculated in the decree moved by Menexenos, the people decreed that the city of Ioulis should repay to Athens the money in the month of Skirophorion during the archonship of Charikleides. If they do not repay it at the prescribed time, let those elected by the people to collect debts collect this debt from the islanders in the best way they know. Let Echetimos, Nikoleos, Satyros, Glaukon, and Herakleides, the generals of Ioulis, assist our collectors. In order to assure the validity of the oaths and alliance which our general Chabrias drafted and swore to the Keans on behalf of the Athenians and of those Keans whom the Athenians restored to Keos, let the generals of Ioulis, mentioned above as assisting in the collection of the money owed to Athens, inscribe the oaths and the alliance on a stele and set it up in the temple of Pythian Apollo, just as the oaths and alliance are recorded in Karthaia. Also, the secretary of the Athenian Council is to inscribe these oaths and the alliance on a stele and set it up on the Acropolis. For this inscription the Treasurer of the People is to pay out twenty drachmas out of the money set aside for decrees. Since some citizens of Ioulis broke the oaths and alliance by making war on the people of Athens, on other Keans and on other allies, and with death already prescribed for returning to Keos, they came back to Keos and threw out the stelai which contained the alliance with Athens and the names of those who had broken the oaths and alliance; since they killed friends of Athens, whom the Athenians had restored to Keos, and also sentenced to death and confiscated the property of Satyridos, Timoxenos, and Miltiades, contrary to the oaths and the alliance, because these three had accused Antipatros when the Council of Athens convicted him of the murder of the Athenian *proxenos* Agaision in violation of the oaths and the alliance and the decrees of Athens: those citizens are therefore to be banished from Keos and Athens, and their property is to be confiscated by the people of Ioulis. The generals of Ioulis who are present at Athens are to record in front of the secretary the names of those men. If anyone whose name is so recorded disputes whether he is one of those men, he may post surety with the generals of Ioulis within thirty days and undergo trial both in Keos and in Athens, at the court chosen for this purpose, in accordance with the oaths and the alliance. Satyridos, Timoxenos, and Miltiades are to be allowed to return to Keos and recover their property. Those who have come from Ioulis — Demetrios, Herakleides, Echetimos, and Kalliphantos — are to be publicly praised. Satyridos, Timoxenos, and Miltiades are also to be publicly praised. The city of Karthaia and Aglaokritos are also to be publicly praised, and all are invited to dine at the Prytaneion tomorrow.

The following are the oaths sworn by Athens and her allies to the cities on Keos: I will bear no grudge towards anyone for the events that happened on Keos, nor will I kill any Kean, nor will I exile any of those who abided by the oaths and the alliance. I will admit them to alliance on the same terms as the other allies. If anyone causes revolution on Keos in violation of the oaths and the alliance, by any device or strategem, I will prevent him to the best of my ability. If anyone desires not to live on Keos, I will permit him to go live wherever he wishes in allied territory and keep his property. I will be true to this oath, by Zeus, Athena, Poseidon, and Demeter. If I keep my oath, may I receive blessings; and curses, if I do not keep it.

Oaths and alliance of the cities on Keos to the Athenians and their allies, and to those Keans whom the Athenians restored: I will be an ally of Athens and her allies. I will not revolt from Athens and her allies and I will prevent anyone else from doing so, to the best of my ability. I will have all civil suits involving an Athenian and a sum of over one hundred drachmas heard before an Athenian court in accordance with the alliance. If anyone dares to injure those who are restored to Keos or the Athenians or their allies in violation of the oaths and the alliance, I will prevent him from doing so by any device or strategem to the best of my ability. I will be true to my oath, by Zeus, Athena, Poseidon, and Demeter. If I keep my oath, may I have blessings; and curses, if I do not keep it.

The following are the oaths sworn by the Keans whom the Athenians restored: I will bear no grudge . . .

45. ATHENS HONORS MENELAOS OF PELAGONIA, 362 B.C.
Tod 143

Since Spartan operations in the North (see No. 18) had stopped, Olynthos had recovered her freedom of action and once again threatened to establish a hegemony in this region. In 364-362 B.C. Athens was fighting in the North for control of Amphipolis (cf. No. 50). In these operations she was allied with Perdikkas III of Macedon and with Pelagonia, a borderland of Macedon; the common enemy was Olynthos and the Chalcidian League.

Menelaos of Pelagonia, a benefactor of Athens. In the archonship of Charikleides (363/2), when Oineis held the sixth prytany (ca. January 362). The Council and the Assembly passed the following decree: Oineis held the prytany, Nikostratos was the secretary, Charikles from Leukonoe presided, and Satyros made the motion: Because the general Timotheos has reported that Menelaos the Pelagonian has contributed war supplies and has himself participated in the war against the Chalcidians and Amphipolis, the Council should vote to present him to the people at its next assembly. At that time the Council should present its resolution to publicly praise Menelaos because he is a worthy man and is doing all he can to benefit the people of Athens. The Council also recommends that the generals in Macedon should take special care in regard to him and supply him with whatever he needs. If Menelaos performs more good services for the people of Athens, the Council assures him that he will find the people grateful. The people should also invite him to dine at the Prytaneion tomorrow. Satyros added this motion: In addition to the Council's recommendation, Menelaos should be titled a benefactor of the people, because Menelaos' ancestors were also titled benefactors of the Athenian people. . . .

[The end is lost.]

46. ALLIANCE OF ATHENS AND PELOPONNESIANS, 362 B.C.
Tod 144

The battle of Mantineia was fought in mid-362 B.C. Thebes and her allies defeated the coalition led by Sparta and Athens, but the victory cost the life of the Theban leader Epameinondas. Without him, Theban policy stagnated and his city soon slipped from its pre-eminent position. The following decree records an alliance between the Athenians, Arcadians, Achaeans, Eleans, and Phleiasians, shortly after the battle.

In the archonship of Molon (362/1). Alliance of the Athenians, Arcadians, Achaeans, Eleans, and Phleiasians. The Council and the Assembly passed the following decree: Oineis held the prytany, Agatharchos son of Agatharchos from Oe was the secretary, Xanthippos from Herme presided, and Periandros made the motion: Let the herald vow to Olympian Zeus, Pallas Athena, Demeter, Kore, the Twelve Gods, and the Erinyes a sacrifice and a procession, if the decision concerning the alliance benefits and everything turns out to the people's wishes. The sacrifice and the procession were vowed when the allies presented a resolution to the Council to accept the alliance on the terms offered by the Arcadians, Achaeans, Eleans, and Phleiasians. The Council recommended acceptance of these terms. The Assembly approved the resolution. The Athenians and their allies, and the Arcadians, Achaeans, Eleans, and Phleiasians are to be allies forever, with good fortune.... If anyone invades Attica or overthrows the democracy of Athens or establishes a tyranny or oligarchy in Athens, the Arcadians, Achaeans, Eleans, and Phleiasians will aid the Athenians in all strength to the best of their ability as the Athenians may request. If anyone invades these cities or overthrows the democracy of Phleious, or if anyone overthrows or changes the governments of the Achaeans, Arcadians, or Eleans, or exiles anyone, the Athenians will aid them with all their strength to the best of their ability as the injured party may request. The supreme command will be held by the state in whose territory the trouble occurred. If all the states agree to add anything to the alliance, it shall be valid under the oaths. The chief magistrates of the Peloponnesians will swear the oath; for the Athenians, the oath will be sworn by the generals, taxiarchs, hipparchs, tribal commanders, and knights...

47. COMMON PEACE OF 362 B.C.: THE STELE OF THE SATRAPS
Tod 154

In this inscription, found at Argos, the Greeks decline a request from the rebel satraps of Persia for aid in their revolt against the King. All the Greek states, except, no doubt, for Sparta who could not suffer the freedom of Messenia, made a fifth Common Peace shortly after the battle of Mantineia in 362 B.C. The satraps' revolt was unsuccessful and was ended by 358 B.C.

[The beginning is lost.]
(It has been decreed) by those Greeks participating in the Common Peace, to explain to the representatives who came from the satraps that the Greeks, having exchanged ambassadors with each other, have surmounted their difficulties and achieved a common peace so that each of the cities is set free from war and now strives for greatness and prosperity in order to render aid to its friends and remain strong. They are not aware of the existence of any state of war between the King and themselves. If he keeps the peace and does not invade Greece and does not seek to break the peace which now exists among us by any device or stratagem,

then we will keep peace with the King. If, however, he makes war against any of our allies or supplies war materials for breaking the peace, or moves against the Greeks who share in the Peace, or if anyone from his territory does so, we will unite to repel him in a manner worthy of the peace we now enjoy and worthy of our past deeds. . . .

[The end is lost.]

48. ATHENS SENDS SETTLERS TO POTEIDAIA, 361 B.C.
Tod 146

Poteidaia had remained independent of Athens since the end of the Peloponnesian War. In 364 B.C., however, Poteidaia was detached from the Olynthian League. According to the following inscription, the desire to strengthen the Athenian element in Poteidaia produced a decision to send out "cleruchs." A cleruch would receive land in Poteidaia and be a citizen of both cities.

In the archonship of Molon (362/1), when Erechtheis held the ninth prytany (ca. May 361), the Council and the Assembly passed the following decree: Erechtheis held the prytany, Agatharchos son of Agatharchos from Oe was secretary, . . . from Kerameis presided, and Philippos made the motion: Concerning the report of those who have come from Poteidaia at public expense, let the people vote as follows: The herald will vow a procession and a sacrifice to the Twelve Gods, the Erinyes, and Herakles, if the decision to send cleruchs to Poteidaia turns out well for the Athenians, in accordance with the report of those who have come from Poteidaia at public expense, and everything turns out to the wishes of the Athenians. . . .

49. ALLIANCE OF ATHENS WITH THESSALY, 361 B.C.
Tod 147

Alexander of Pherai had attempted to recover the power once held by Jason (No. 27). Thebes and Macedon were successful in thwarting his ambitions (see No. 36) until the death of Epameinondas at Mantineia in 362 B.C. With Thebes no longer able to intervene in Thessaly, the other Thessalians turned to Athens; Athens, previously allied with Alexander, was also eager for this alliance because he had executed raids on Athenian allies and defeated an Athenian fleet.

Gods. In the archonship of Nikophemos (361/0). Alliance without time-limit between the Athenians and the Thessalians. The Council and the Assembly passed the following decree: Leontis held the prytany, Chairon son of Charinautos from Phaleron was the secretary, and Archippos from Amphitrope presided. On the twelfth day of the prytany Exekestides made the following motion: Concerning the report of the Thessalian ambassadors, the Assembly should vote to accept the alliance, with hope of good fortune, on the terms offered. There will be an alliance without time-limit between them and the Athenians. The allies of the Athenians are all to be allies of the Thessalians, and the allies of the Thessalians are all to be allies of the Athenians. The generals, the Council, the hipparchs, and the knights of Athens are to swear the following oath: I will help the Thessalians with all my strength to the utmost of my ability if anyone invades the territory of the Thessalian League or overthrows the archon whom the Thessalians have elected or establishes a tyranny in Thessaly. They are then to swear the customary oath. To receive the oaths from the Thessalians, the Assembly will elect five men from all the Athenians to go to Thessaly and administer the oath to the archon Agelaos, to the polemarchs, the hipparchs, the knights, the sacred officials, and all the other magistrates who hold office for the League. The oath is as follows: I will aid the Athenians will all my strength to the utmost of my ability if anyone attacks the city of Athens with warlike intent or overthrows the democracy of Athens. The Thessalian ambassadors who are now in Athens are to swear this same oath. The war against Alexander is not to be stopped either by the Thessalians without the Athenians or by the Athenians without the archon and the League of the Thessalians. The archon Agelaos and the League of the Thessalians are to be publicly praised because they have done enthusiastically and well everything the city requested. Also, the Thessalian ambassadors who are present are to be publicly praised and invited to dine at the Prytaneion tomorrow.

The Treasurers of Athena are to destroy the stele containing the alliance with Alexander. The Treasurer of the People is to give each of the ambassadors twenty drachmas for travel expenses. The secretary of the Council is to record this alliance on a stone stele and erect it on the Acropolis. He is to allow thirty drachmas for this stele. Theaitetos from Erchia is to be considered as having acted quite properly, speaking and acting to accomplish the greatest possible good for the Athenians and the Thessalians.

50. MACEDON CAPTURES AMPHIPOLIS, 357 B.C.
Tod 150

Macedon was an ill-united kingdom and a weak state in a region which was desirable and strategically important. The stronger Greek states were generally active in the North. Macedon survived by playing one off against the other. Macedon's weakness was ended in 359 B.C., and ended by one man, the new king Philip II. His brother Perdikkas III (365-359 B.C.) had already done much to strengthen the kingdom. Philip reorganized its fighting forces; he was probably the first to arm the peasants as infantry, creating the famous Macedonian phalanx. He had learnt much about war while a hostage at Thebes in the days of Epameinondas and Pelopidas. He brought to his leadership of Macedon a measure of drive and determination reminiscent of the portrait of Jason (No. 27). His energy made Macedon into a first-rate power, gave her control of the North from Thessaly to Thrace, and finally made her mistress of all Greece (No. 73). His first contact as king with Athens came shortly after his accession, when Athens supported rivals for his throne; Philip defeated the expedition and generously returned the Athenian captives. In 357 B.C., he attacked Amphipolis; men spoke of a secret pact under which Philip was to give the city to Athens. In any case he kept it for himself. Under his control, Amphipolis passed the following decree of banishment against Stratokles, who had come to Athens for aid when Philip was attacking Amphipolis, and a Philon, otherwise unknown.

The people decreed as follows: Philon and Stratokles are condemned to permanent exile from the city and territory of Amphipolis, both themselves and their children. If they are captured, they are to be punished as traitors and killed with impunity. Their goods are to be confiscated, and a tithe will be dedicated to the god Apollo and to the god of the Strymon River. The presiding officers are to inscribe their names on a stone stele.

If anyone attempts to annul this decree, or if anyone gives aid of any sort to the outlaws, he will have his goods confiscated and he will be exiled from Amphipolis.

51. SETTLEMENT BETWEEN ATHENS AND THE KINGS OF THRACE, 357 B.C.
Tod 151

In the North, Athens had to reckon with Macedon, Amphipolis, Olynthos, and the Kingdom of Thrace. Kotys I (383-359 B.C.) was long friendly to Athens; he had even married his daughter to the general Iphikrates. In 362 B.C., however, Athens had failed to support him, and he retaliated by invading the Chersonese, which was allied with Athens and was important for Athens' wheat imports. Kotys was assassinated in 359 B.C., and his death increased Athens' difficulties, because there were three successors to his throne. After a period of indecisive negotiations and hostilities, the following treaty was struck. In it, Athens and the three kings recognize each other's claims to the Chersonese. Thrace became subject to Macedon in the next decade, and Philip's attack on Kersebleptes in 352 B.C. was what first seriously alarmed Demosthenes to the threat of Macedon.

[The beginning is gone.]
... if any of the cities, whose names are inscribed on the stelai and pay tribute to either Berisades, or Amadokos, or Kersebleptes and also pay tribute to Athens, does not pay its tribute to Athens, then Berisades, Amadokos, and Kersebleptes will to the best of their ability compel it to do so. If, also, any of these cities does not pay its tribute to either Berisades or Amadokos or Kersebleptes, then Athens and the officials in office at the time will to the best of their ability compel it to do so. The Greek cities in the Chersonese which pay the customary tribute to Berisades, Amadokos, and Kersebleptes and also pay Confederacy-dues to the Athenians will be free and autonomous, because they are allies of the Athenians according to the oaths they swore and also of Berisades, Amadokos, and Kersebleptes. If any of these cities revolts from Athens, Berisades and Amadokos and Kersebleptes will give help as the Athenians may request. And if ...
[The end is lost.]

52. ALLIANCE OF ATHENS AND EUBOIAN CITIES, 357/6 B.C.
Tod 153

The island of Euboia was of great importance to Athens. It was a source of grain, meat, and hides; most importantly, Euboia was a key point for controlling the route of the ships which brought grain to Athens from the Black Sea. The cities of Euboia were members of the fifth century empire of Athens, and their revolt in 411 B.C. was a serious blow. They joined the Second Athenian Confederacy (Nos. 22 and 23), but were great supporters of Thebes during her hegemony. In 357/6 B.C. political strife in some of the cities of Euboia led Thebes to invade; Athenian forces repelled the invasion, and took advantage of the opportunity to renew contacts with the cities, as indicated by this inscription.

[The beginning is lost.]
... this decree is to be published on the Acropolis by the secretary of the current prytany. The Treasurer will pay the money from the funds budgeted for decrees. Five men are to be elected to travel and receive the oaths from the citizens of Karystos. The taxiarchs, the generals, and the Council are to swear the oaths to the Karystians. The people of Karystos are to be publicly praised; their ambassadors and their representative to the Confederacy are also to be publicly praised and invited to dine tomorrow at the Prytaneion. The general Menes and the ambassadors sent to Karystos are also to be publicly praised and invited to dine at the Prytaneion tomorrow. The Treasurer of the People will give each of the envoys travel expenses of twenty drachmas out of the money budgeted for decrees. The Treasurer of the People will also give travel expenses of twenty drachmas each to those who were ambassadors to Eretria, Chalkis, and Hestiaia. The Treasurer of the People will also give ten drachmas to each of those who negotiated the alliance. The following swore the oath: the Council in the archonship of Agathokles (357/6); the generals Chabrias from Aixone, Chares from Angele, Iphikrates from Rhamnous, Menon from Potamos, Philochares from Rhamnous, Exekestides from Thorikos, Alkimachos from Anagyrous, and Diokles from Alopeke.

53. ATHENIAN HELP TO ERETRIA, 357/6 B.C.
Tod 154

As a result of the disturbances on Euboia (No. 52), the following decree was passed. It provides the legal machinery for handling similar occurrences. The case of Eretria set a precedent for handling aggression within the Second Athenian Confederacy as an internal affair fully covered by the laws of the League.

Decree of the Assembly. Hegesippos made the motion: In order that no one, whether Athenian or anyone else, foreigner or citizen, whether invading from Attica or from any allied city, may ever again injure any of the allies, the people should vote as follows: Concerning those who invaded the territory of Eretria, the Council recommended to the people at the very next assembly that those people should be punished in accordance with the treaty. If anyone ever again invades Eretria or any other allied city, either that of Athens herself or of one of her allies, he will be punished with death, and his property will be confiscated, with a tithe going to Athena. All his property owned in any allied city will be liable to confiscation. If any city refuses to surrender his property, that city will owe its value to the Confederacy. This law will be inscribed on a stone stele and erected on the Acropolis, in the Agora, and in the harbor. The Treasurer of the People will allot money for the inscribing. Public praise will be given to those who rendered aid to Eretria, . . . the Karystians . . . and the general . . .

[The end is lost.]

54. THE SOCIAL WAR:
A HISTORIAN IN COMMAND AT ARKESINE, 357/6 B.C.
Tod 152

Athens had constructed her Second Confederacy with care (No. 22), hoping to avoid the practices which had tarnished the image of her fifth century empire. Allies, nevertheless, became dissatisfied and attempted to leave the Confederacy (Nos. 31, 44); some shifted their alliance to the stronger Thebes during the period of the Theban hegemony (Nos. 42, 52). A very serious threat to the Confederacy came in 357 B.C. when Chios, Kos, Rhodes, and Byzantium seceded with the support of Maussollos (No. 40) and formed a counter-alliance with each other. The Confederacy determined to crush the revolt and thus began the "Social War" of 357-355 B.C. This war was fought chiefly through naval campaigns in the Aegean. The rebels had a strong combined fleet, and Athens was required not only to attack it, but also to defend the remaining allies against attack. The Confederacy thus had recourse to the installation of garrisons in exposed cities, a measure forbidden by the Decree of Aristoteles (No. 22). In the following inscription we see the Atthidographer Androtion in command at Arkesine on the island of Amorgos. See also Nos. 55 and 56.

The Council and Assembly of Arkesine passed the following decree: since Androtion has behaved nobly toward the people of Arkesine, and, when he was governor of the city he did not harm any citizen or any foreigner who came to the city; and since he did not wish to charge interest on the money which he lent to the city in a time of need; and because he made up from his own money the pay owed to the garrison, and he charged no interest when the money was repaid at the year's end; and because he saved the city twelve minas per year and ransomed many who were captured by the enemy, therefore Androtion son of Andron of Athens should be crowned with a gold crown worth five hundred drachmas because of his virtue, justice, and kindness towards the people of Arkesine. He will be titled *proxenos* and benefactor of the city of Arkesine, both himself and his descendants, and he will be freed from all our taxes. Because the allies thus decreed . . .

[The end is lost.]

55. THE SOCIAL WAR: ANDROS GARRISONED, 356 B.C.
Tod 156

This decree presents a case similar to the preceding. The Confederacy had decided to post a guard on the island of Andros; this decree specifies that an Athenian general should supervise it. The Confederacy as a whole pays for the garrison from its dues; Arkesine, on the other hand, was apparently responsible for supporting its garrison.

In the archonship of Agathokles (357/6), when Aigeis held the ninth prytany (ca. May 356), Diodotos son of Diokles from Angele was secretary, and the *proedros* Diotimos from Oinoe put the vote, the Council and the Assembly passed the following decree, moved by Hegesandros: In order that Andros may be kept safe for the people of Athens and for the people of Andros, in order that the garrison on Andros may receive its pay from the Confederacy-dues according to the decrees of the allies, and so that the garrison may not be dissolved, one of the men elected as general should be appointed to take charge of Andros. Archedemos is to collect the money from the islands which is owed to the soldiers in Andros and give it to the governor of Andros, so that the soldiers may have their pay . . .

[The end is lost.]

56. PROVISIONS FOR KEOS, CA. 356 B.C.
IG II² 404

This decree appears to once again re-establish or confirm the alliance of Athens with the cities in Keos. It may therefore indicate the occurrence of troubles similar to those recorded in No. 44. The phrase "in order that Keos be kept safe," etc., suggests that Keos is to be garrisoned, and that this inscription belongs together with Nos. 54 and 55. Chabrias died in battle at Keos in 357 B.C. The 2 per cent tax mentioned in the inscription was a customs-duty levied by Athens on goods passing through Peiraieus.

[The preamble and the beginning of the decree are fragmentary.]

. . . Concerning the lawful supplication . . . and Simalos and . . . in order that Keos may be kept safe for the people of Athens and for the cities in Keos, the cities in Keos . . . entered the *synhedrion* . . . and the name of each city was inscribed on the stele and Confederacy-dues have been assessed. The Assembly has decreed to validate the oaths and alliance which the general Chabrias made with the cities in Keos. The cities in Keos shall govern themselves as individual cities according to the oaths, the alliance, and the decrees of the people of Athens. The cities on the coast shall be fortified. If Athens has any complaint with them concerning arrears of the 2% tax, the Keans shall undergo arbitration at Athens and in the *synhedrion*, according to the oaths, the alliance, and the decrees of the Athenian people. . . .

[The end is lost.]

57. ATHENS MAKES ALLIANCE WITH NORTHERN KINGS, 356 B.C.
Tod 157

Faced with the expansion of Macedon, three kings from Illyria, Paionia, and Thrace made an alliance with Athens. Diodorus (16.22.3) mentions their mutual alliance but omits Athens; Athens, no doubt, could not aid them very much at this time, because she was having trouble in Euboia (Nos. 52 and 53) and was fighting the Social War. Ketriporis and his brothers may have been sons of Berisades (No. 51), who died in 357/6 B.C. Krenides was a colony of Thasos which appealed to Philip for help against the Thracians. He sent troops to garrison it and changed its name to Philippi (see No. 59).

Lysias son of Lys. . . from Pithos was the secretary. Alliance of Athens with Ketriporis and his brothers, with Lyppeios the Paionian, and with Grabos the Illyrian. In the archonship of Elpines (356/5), on the eleventh day of the first prytany (ca. early July 356) with Hippothontis holding the prytany; the *proedros* Mnesarchos put the vote. The Council and Assembly passed the following decree, on the motion of Kallisthenes: May good fortune come to the people of Athens; let them accept the alliance on the terms reported by Monounios the brother of Ketriporis. Monounios said that these terms were approved by his brother and the ambassador whom Athens sent to Ketriporis and his brothers, to Lyppeios the Paionian, and to Grabos the Illyrian. The *proedroi* of the first assembly should present to the people Monounios the brother of Ketriporis, Peisianax, the ambassadors who were sent by Lyppeios and Grabos, and . . . , who has come from Chares. Let the Council then present to the people its opinion that the alliance is in the best interests of Athens. . . . Let Ketriporis and his brothers be publicly praised, because they are men who help the people of Athens. Let Monounios the brother of Ketriporis, who has come from Ketriporis, also be publicly praised, because of his virtue and good will. Let him be invited to dine at the Prytaneion tomorrow. Let Peisianax also be publicly praised and invited to dine at the Prytaneion tomorrow. Let the ambassadors from the other kings also be invited to dine at the Prytaneion tomorrow. If this decree is deficient in any respect, the Council is empowered to amend it.

The following have been chosen ambassadors: Lysikrates from Oinoe, Antimachos . . . , . . . , Thrason from Erchia.

I swear, by Zeus, Earth, Sun, Poseidon, Athena, and Ares, that I will be a friend and ally to Ketriporis and his brothers, and that I will fight faithfully in war against Philip with all my strength to the best of my ability. I will not cease fighting Philip before Ketriporis and his brothers cease fighting. I will assist Ketriporis and his brothers to capture the land which Philip now holds, and I will help Ketriporis and his brothers to capture Krenides, and I will restore . . .

[The end is lost.]

58. ALLIANCE BETWEEN PHILIP AND OLYNTHOS, 356 B.C.
Tod 158

Philip's capture of Amphipolis (No. 50) made him a grave threat to Olynthos and her Chalcidian League. Athens refused to make an alliance with Olynthos, and Olynthos was therefore driven to make terms with Philip. He immediately rewarded her for this alliance by giving her Anthemos and Poteidaia. By this time there was no doubt that Philip was the main power in the North; he had a well-trained army and access to the gold mines between Amphipolis and Philippi. No other state was now involved in the area: Athens was detained by her troubles in Euboia and by the Social War; Thebes was concerned with Euboia and Phokis (see No. 60); Alexander of Pherai (No. 49) was dead; and Sparta was now too weak to venture outside the Peloponnese.

[The preamble and beginning are lost.]

The magistrates and representatives of the Chalcidian League are to swear the oaths to Philip; Philip and any others designated by the Chalcidians are to swear the oaths to the Chalcidians. Both parties are to swear without guile or artifice by Zeus, Earth, Sun, and Poseidon, with the invocation of blessings on him who swears truly and curses on him who does not. This treaty and the oracle which the god gave concerning the alliance are to be inscribed by the Chalcidians on a stele and erected in the temple of Artemis in Olynthos. Philip is to erect a stele with these documents inscribed on it in the temple of Zeus at Dion. Both the Chalcidians and Philip are to set up at Delphi a copy of the stele and the oracle. There is to be a three-month period in which changes mutually agreeable to Philip and the Chalcidians may be made.

The god prophesied to the Chalcidians and to Philip that it would be beneficial and good for them to be friends and allies on the terms as agreed. Sacrifices are to be made and omens taken in the names of Zeus Supreme and Perfect, of Apollo the Protector, of Artemis Orthosia, and of Hermes. Good fortune. Vows are to be made for the endurance of the alliance, thanks are to be paid to Pythian Apollo, and public thanksgivings are to be made.

59. ATHENS DEALS WITH NEAPOLIS, 355 B.C.
Tod 159

Neapolis is on the coast of Thrace opposite the island of Thasos. It had been a member of the Fifth-Century Empire and had remained loyal after the disaster at Syracuse (see Meiggs-Lewis 89 = Tod 84 = *IG* I^2 108 +). It joined the Second Athenian Confederacy (cf. No. 22) and remained loyal during the Social War, as shown by this inscription. The content of the decree is unfortunately all lost; any guess as to its sense would be vain, although the activities of Philip would be the main problem in this region. Chares made Neapolis an Athenian naval base in 354 B.C., but it fell to Philip, who needed a seaport for Philippi (No. 57).

The Social War went badly for Athens and the Confederacy. Naval campaigns in 357 and 356 B.C. left the rebels solidly entrenched; the general Chares earned some much-needed money by assisting a rebel satrap, but this action brought strong protests and threats from the Persian Emperor. The War was ended late in 355 B.C. by a treaty which granted the secession of the rebel states, and the Confederacy was greatly weakened. Rhodes, Kos, and Chios were soon subjugated by their ally Maussollos.

In the archonship of Elpines (356/5). (Honors for) the Neapolitans Demosthenes son of Theoxenos, and Dioskourides son of Ameipsias. Antiochis held the ninth prytany (ca. May 355), Lysias son of Lys... was secretary, and the *proedros* Kallistogeiton from Phegaia put the vote. The Council and Assembly approved the motion of Polyeuktos: Concerning the report of Demosthenes and Dioskourides, the ambassadors from Neapolis, the *proedroi* at the next assembly are to present these ambassadors to the people and negotiate the matters in their report. The Council shall report to the people its recommendation that, since the Assembly has voted ...

[The rest is too fragmentary.]

60. THE THIRD SACRED WAR: RECORD OF CONTRIBUTIONS, 355-51 B.C.
Tod 160

The operations of the sanctuary of Apollo at Delphi were supervised by the Delphian Amphictyony. This was an extremely ancient council made up of representatives from twelve Greek tribes, dedicated to preserving the shrine as inviolable and open to all, and to enforcing good behavior among the member tribes. The First Sacred War occurred in 591/0 B.C. against the Phokian city of Kirrha, which was attempting to claim Delphi. Kirrha was destroyed and its territory declared sacred (i.e. dedicated to Apollo and not to be used for any human purpose such as grazing or cultivation). The Second Sacred War, in the middle of the fifth century B.C. involved Athens and Sparta in a struggle to place Delphi in the control of their supporters. The Third Sacred War broke out in 356 B.C. because the Thebans persuaded the Amphictyony to levy a crushing fine upon Phokis over some infraction. Phokis in desperate retaliation seized Delphi itself, which was excellent as a strategic position against Thebes; the Phokians also used the treasures of the sanctuary to support their army. Branded as temple-robbers, the Phokians suffered through eleven years of a war which convulsed all of Greece. Out of hostility to Thebes, Athens and Sparta supported Phokis.

Because Phokis had seized Delphi, Thebes had to receive contributions from those who wished to support the Sacred War. The following inscription from Thebes lists such contributors. Alyzeia and Anaktorion had deserted Athens in 362; Byzantium was at war with Athens; Tenedos remained loyal to Athens, but the Boeotian *proxenos* in Tenedos gave a very large amount.

The following contributed for the war which the Boeotians are waging on behalf of the temple at Delphi against those who are desecrating the shrine of Pythian Apollo.

During the archonship (at Thebes) of Aristion:

Alyzeia (The envoys were Charops son of Dadon and Arist . . . .)	. . .
Anaktorion (The envoys were Phormo and Arkos Teireios)	30 minas
Byzantium (Members of the Council of Byzantium brought the contribution: Kerkinos son of Heirotimos, Ag. . . son of Deloptichos, Dionysios son of Heiraion, Athenodoros son of Dionysios)	84 gold Lampsakene staters, 16 silver Attic drachmas
The Boeotian *proxenos* in Tenedos	1,000 drachmas

During the archonship of Nikolaos:

Alyzeia (The envoys were Theo. . . son of Alexandros, and Dion son of Poly. . .)	another 30 minas

During the archonship of Agesinikos:

Byzantium (The contribution for the war being waged by the Boeotians on behalf of the temple at Delphi was brought by members of the Council: Sosis son of Karatichos, and Parmeniskos son of Pyramos)	500 gold staters

61. ATHENS RENEWS MONOPOLY ON OCHER FROM KEOS, BEFORE 350 B.C.
Tod 162

This inscription is an Athenian copy of laws passed by Karthaia, Koresos, and Ioulis, the cities on the island of Keos. Ocher is an iron oxide which was in great demand as a pigment for red and yellow paint and as the basis for a drug. The decrees assure Athens exclusive access to Kean ocher and promise large rewards for information or prosecution of lawbreakers. For other relations of Athens and Keos see Nos. 44 and 56. The 2 per cent tax was also mentioned in No. 56.

[The Karthaian decree is too badly preserved to translate.]

The motion of Theogenes was approved by the Council and Assembly of Koresos: Concerning the report of the envoys from Athens, Athens will be allowed to export ocher on the same terms as before. In order to maintain the decrees previously passed by Athens and Koresos concerning the ocher, it will be exported in whatever ship the Athenians may designate, but in no other ship. The freight charge will be one obol per talent of ocher, paid to the ship-owners by the producers. If anyone exports ocher in any other ship, he will be liable. ... Let this decree be inscribed on a stone stele and erected in the temple of Apollo, and the law will be valid as it was before. Charges of law-breaking are to be reported to the *astynomoi*, who are to bring the matter into court within thirty days. To the complainant or informer will come half ... (if he is a free man?); if the informer is a slave and belongs to the shippers, he will be freed and receive three-quarters of the amount involved; if he belongs to someone else, he will be freed and ... An informer or complainant may have appeal to Athens. If the Athenians pass any other decree concerning the protection of the ocher, it will take effect as soon as it arrives here. The producers are to pay the two per cent tax to those in charge of collecting it. Let the Athenians be invited to dine at the Prytaneion tomorrow.

The Council and People of Ioulis passed the following decree: Concerning the report of the Athenian envoys, the Council and Assembly of Ioulis have decided that from this day on ocher may be exported to Athens, but to no other city. If anyone exports it elsewhere, his ship and goods will be confiscated. Half will be given to the informer or complainant. If he is a slave, he will be freed and receive ... of the goods. The shipper will transport his ocher in a ship designated by the Athenians; if anyone ships it in any other ship, he will be liable for ... If the Athenians pass any other decrees concerning the export of ocher, these decrees will be valid here. There will be exemption from the ... tax after the month Hermaion. Let the Athenians be invited to dine at the Prytaneion. Complaints will be reported to the Eleven at Athens and to the *prostatai* at Ioulis. If anyone exports ocher in violation of the law, half of his goods will be given to the people of Ioulis and half to the informer. This decree is to be inscribed by the Council and erected in the harbor.

The following were chosen (i.e. are the Athenian envoys): Andron from Kerameis, Lysia..., ... from Phlya, Euphrosynos from Paiania.

62. LEUKON GRANTS TRADE PRIVILEGES TO MYTILENE, ABOUT 350 B.C.
Tod 163

Leukon was the ruler of the Bosporan Kingdom, centered in the Crimea. This region was extremely important to Greece because it exported large quantities of wheat. Mytilene had left the Second Athenian Confederacy as a result of the Social War. In this inscription Leukon grants a reduction of the tax he imposed on wheat exported to Mytilene. The condition of the stone (only one sentence is really readable) makes it difficult to be sure about the new terms; they are, however, certainly a favor, because the normal tax was one-thirtieth (3.3%). A *medimnos* equals 1 1/2 bushels. Athens paid no tax at all because of the vast amounts which they imported and the honors which they paid to the Bosporan Kings (see No. 65).

Leukon and his sons have granted to the Mytileneans that they may pay a simple tax on wheat of one-sixtieth (1.7%) and one-ninetieth (1.1%) on quantities up to 100,000 *medimnoi*.

63. TREATY BETWEEN ERYTHRAI AND HERMEIAS OF ATARNEUS, ABOUT 350 B.C.
Tod 165

Hermeias was tyrant of Atarneus, which is on the coast of Asia opposite Mytilene. Erythrai was a Greek city to the south, near to Chios. Both parties are part of the Persian Empire, but considerable independence of action was usual under all but the most scrupulous emperors. In this inscription the two cities make a mutual alliance and arrange for the mutual safe-keeping of property.

Hermeias, a student of Plato's Academy and a close friend of Aristotle, was executed by Persia in 341 B.C. for treacherous dealings with Macedon.

[The beginning is lost.]

... if the Erythraians should deposit anything in the territory of Hermeias and his companions because of war, all of it and any income produced by it will be untaxed, except if anything is sold. If anything is sold, a 2% tax on it will be paid. Whenever peace is restored, the property will be sent back within three days. If it is not sent back, taxes will be levied. The property will be deposited after a fair declaration of it. If Hermeias and his companions wish to deposit anything (here), they may do so in the same way. The Erythraians are to swear their oath to Hermeias and his companions. The oath is as follows: I will aid Hermeias and his companions on land and on sea with all my strength to the best of my ability, and I will accomplish everything according to the agreement. The generals will supervise the taking of the oaths, in co-operation with ambassadors from Hermeias and his companions. Perfect sacrifices will be made, and the city will pay for the victims. Hermeias and his companions will likewise swear to aid the Erythraians on land and on sea with all their strength to the best of their ability, and to accomplish everything according to the agreement. They will swear by the usual gods. This treaty will be inscribed on a stone stele and set up in the shrine of Athena by the Erythraians, and in the shrine of (the eponymous hero) Atarneus by Hermeias.

64. PHILIP DESTROYS OLYNTHOS, 348 B.C.
Tod 166

Philip and Olynthos had become allies in 356 B.C. (No. 58) and Philip benefitted his ally with continued favors. Many Olynthians remained suspicious of Philip, and the city became disloyal when Philip was far away attacking Kersebleptes (see No. 51) in 352 B.C. Philip attacked Olynthos soon afterwards, and the Athenian politician Demosthenes, convinced that Philip was the most dangerous power in the world, pleaded with the Athenians to help Olynthos. Athens did not send enough help in time and Olynthos fell to Philip in 348 B.C., betrayed from within. Philip razed the city and dissolved the Chalcidian League, leaving the cities in the area completely subject to himself. The following Athenian inscription describes the reception and relief granted to Olynthian refugees at Athens.

[The beginning is lost.]
... Concerning the decision of the Olynthians to become lawful suppliants of the people of Athens and of the allies: because the Olynthians had become allies of Athens and of her allies and were then driven by siege out of their city by Philip, and they now request to be exempted from the tax on resident aliens at Athens, let the people immediately vote on whether or not it will grant exemption from the tax on resident aliens to the Olynthian refugees. If the people vote to give them this exemption, let the secretary of the Council inscribe their names on a stone stele, and also that they were besieged out of their city by Philip. Let the cost of the stele ...
[The rest is lost.]

65. ATHENS HONORS THE SONS OF LEUKON, 346 B.C.
Tod 167

The realm of Leukon (No. 62) was Athens' chief source of wheat. Leukon died in 346 B.C. and was succeeded by two of his sons, Spartokos and Pairisades, who immediately confirmed the previous relations with Athens. In the following decree, emphasis is laid on the honors given to the two kings, their titles, and the gifts given to Athena in their name. Apollonios, mentioned in the rider, is known only from this inscription. The proposer Androtion is the same man as in No. 54.

For Spartokos, Pairisades, and Apollonios, the sons of Leukon. In the archonship of Themistokles (347/6), when Aigeis held the eighth prytany (ca. April 346), Lysimachos son of Sosidemos from Acharne was secretary, and Theophilos from Halimous presided, Androtion son of Andron from Gargettos made the following motion: Concerning the report of Spartokos, Pairisades, and their ambassadors, let the following reply be made. The people of Athens praises Spartokos and Pairisades for their goodness in announcing to the people of Athens that they will care for the exportation of grain to Athens just as their father used to do, and that they will willingly render military aid whenever the people need it. Let the ambassadors announce to them that if they do these things they will never have bad fortune as far as the people of Athens are concerned. Because they are giving to Athens the same gifts which their grandfather Satyros and their father Leukon gave to Athens, the people of Athens will give to Spartokos and Pairisades the same gifts which were given to Satyros and Leukon. They will also be crowned at the Great Panathenaian festival with a crown of one thousand drachmas each. The crowns will be made by the Athlothetai in the year before the Great Panathenaia, in accordance with the decree which the people of Athens voted for Leukon. It shall be announced that the people of Athens crowns Spartokos and Pairisades the sons of Leukon because of their excellence and good will towards the people of Athens. When they dedicate the crowns to Pallas Athena, the Athlothetai will set up the crowns in the temple with the inscription: Spartokos and Pairisades the sons of Leukon dedicate these crowns, with which the people of Athens crowned them, to Athena. The Treasurer of the People will give to the Athlothetai the money for the crowns out of the money budgeted for decrees. For the immediate occasion the Athlothetai will pay for the crowns out of the Soldier's Fund. Let the secretary of the Council inscribe this decree on a stone stele and erect it near the stele which honors Satyros and Leukon. Let the Treasurer of the People pay out thirty drachmas for the inscribing. The ambassadors Sosis and Theodosios are to be praised for taking care of those who arrived at the Bosporos from Athens. They are to be invited to dine at the Prytaneion tomorrow. Concerning the money owed to the sons of Leukon and how it shall be repaid, let those who may be *proedroi* on the eighteenth day after the sacrifices handle the matter so that the kings will have no complaint when they receive the money from the Athenians. They will be given the adjutants as they request; let the names of those whom they take be recorded with the secretary of the Council by the ambassadors. The men who are so recorded will be considered to be acting quite properly in doing their utmost to help the sons of Leukon. Polyeuktos son of Timokrates from Krioa made the following motion: Let everything proposed by Androtion be approved, but also let Apollonios the son of Leukon be crowned in the same way.

66. MYTILENE REJOINS THE ATHENIAN CONFEDERACY, 346 B.C.
Tod 168

The defection of Mytilene from the Confederacy seems to have coincided with revolutions on that island which resulted in an oligarchy and, next, a tyranny coming into power. The overthrow of the tyrant was followed by the application of the restored democracy to once again become an ally of Athens. The Paralos and the Salaminia were the two Athenian state triremes, reserved for admiralty work and important dispatches.

In the archonship of Themistokles (347/6) the Council and Assembly passed the following decree. Aigeis held the prytany, Lysimachos son of Sosidemos from Acharne was secretary, and Theophilos from Halimous presided. Stephanos son of Antidorides proposed the motion: Concerning the reports of the Mytilenean ambassador, of the steward of the Paralos, and of the general Phaidros, let the people decree that friendship and alliance exist between Mytilene and Athens on the same terms as exist between Athens and other cities. The money from the Confederacy-dues which is allotted to Mytilene . . .

[The end is lost.]

67. PEACE OF PHILOKRATES, 346 B.C.
Demosthenes 19.19-24

The exact truth about who betrayed whom in the Peace of Philokrates will never be known. All of the evidence is biased, and most of it portrays Athens as the wronged party. Athens had technically been at war with Macedon since 357 B.C. when Philip refused to surrender Amphipolis as he, according to the Athenians, was supposed to do (see No. 50). Athens' influence since then had been steadily declining, as Philip consolidated his power in the north, destroying the Chalcidian League (see No. 64) and threatening Athens' corn supply; at the same time Euboia fell from the Athenian alliance. And in 347 B.C. Thebes called on Philip to end the Sacred War (see No. 69). Word, however, reached Athens that Philip wished to come to terms with Athens.

Ten ambassadors were sent to Philip; the most prominent were Philokrates, Aeschines and Demosthenes. The first two represented the policy of drawing close to Macedon to prevent Thebes from becoming predominant in central Greece. It also seems that Philokrates, the chief ambassador of the Athenians and after whom the Peace is named, was on Philip's payroll. Demosthenes, however, pursued an anti-Macedonian policy and wished to draw close to Thebes so that both could resist Macedonian advances into central Greece.

The following excerpt, from Demosthenes' speech when he accused Aeschines of treason, lists some of the reasons why the Athenians voted for the peace. No doubt Aeschines did say these things would be done, and perhaps Philip did intend to do some of them. Philip had no need of a strong Thebes who would control Delphi and probably intrigue in Thessaly which Philip now controlled.

But Philip did not humble Thebes, nor did he destroy the Boeotian League, nor return Oropos or Euboia to Athens. The peace concluded between Philip and Athens did not specifically state what actions Philip or Athens was to take. Peace was concluded on the status quo. Only Athens and her allies in the Second Confederacy were guaranteed their territorial holdings.

Athens was, however, bitterly disappointed in the Peace, because no material advantage came to her as she expected and thought Philip had indicated. Phokis and Kersebleptes, the king of Thrace, who were not members of the Second Confederacy, but were favored by Athens, were treated at Philip's discretion. Perhaps because Philip could not trust Athens with its vocal anti-Macedonian policy, Philip instead drew closer to Thebes in the settlement of the Phokian affair and finally pensioned Kersebleptes off as he took control of all of Thrace. Athens, once more guaranteed the Chersonese, felt nevertheless her corn supply threatened. Minor M. Markle, *The Peace of Philocrates* (Princeton dissertation, 1967), furnishes an excellent analysis of the complicated diplomacy surrounding this treaty.

... But he (Aeschines) delivered such a speech, promising so many things, that he carried you all away with him. He said that he had persuaded Philip to do what was in the interest of Athens both in the Amphictyonic question and in everything else. He then made a long speech denouncing the Thebans, the same speech he said he had given to Philip himself, only that here he was recapitulating just the main points. He also gave as a reasonable estimate that because of his diplomacy you would within two or three days, even though you remain at home not going on campaign and not worrying, hear that Thebes, the city alone, was being blockaded, while the rest of Boeotia remained unmolested, that Thespiai and Plataia were once again being settled, and that Apollo's treasure had been recovered, not from the Phokians, but from the Thebans who had been planning to seize the sanctuary. Aeschines said that he himself had informed Philip that those who planned to seize Delphi were as guilty as those who actually seized the sanctuary. Because of this, he told us, the Thebans had even set a price on his head. He said that he even heard some Euboeans, utterly frightened at the thought of friendship between Philip and Athens, say, "Ambassadors, we know what the terms are for the peace treaty between Philip and Athens. We know that you have renounced your claim to Amphipolis and that Philip has agreed to give Euboia to you." Aeschines also said that another matter had been settled, but that it was better not to mention it just yet — some of his colleagues were jealous of him. He was hinting at Oropos. After disclosing all this, when everyone thought he was a wonderful speaker and someone to be admired, he descended from the rostrum like a king. Then I rose and said that I didn't know anything about what he said, and I tried to repeat what I had said to the Council. Aeschines and Philokrates, standing on either side of me, shouted, interrupted and finally jeered at me. You all laughed: neither did you want to listen to me nor believe anything except what Aeschines had reported. All this is perfectly understandable: how could anyone, thinking he was going to have all this done for him, tolerate a speaker who told you that none of this would happen.

68. ACCOUNTS OF THE DELPHIAN SANCTUARY, 346-344 B.C.
Tod 169

In 346 B.C. the Sacred War was ended by the Phokian surrender (No. 67). As a result of the settlement, the Delphians became full members of the Amphictyony and took full charge of the sanctuary (for the other results see No. 69). In the following inscription we have the accounts of the curators of the sanctuary (*naopoioi*) after the Phokians had abandoned Delphi. The first two sums mentioned represent money entrusted to the Delphians by the pre-war naopoioi, which the Delphians seem to have successfully protected from the Phokians; the Delphians now begin to restore it to the accounts of the temple. Expenditures in the autumn of 346 B.C., immediately after the war, are at a minimum. In 345 B.C. and after, money is spent paying the salaries of the normal employees, cleaning and restoring the sanctuary. Onomarchos and Philomelos, whose statues are recorded as removed, were Phokian generals during the occupation of Delphi. The currency is in the Aeginetan standard.

Statement of money received during the spring term in the archonship of Damoxenos (345 B.C.)

From the 3,404 Aeginetan drachmas and 1 obol, which the naopoioi entrusted to the Delphians during the war, we paid to acounts receivable	1,877 dr., 5 ob.
From 74,670 Aeginetan drachmas likewise due from Delphi to the naopoioi, we paid to acounts receivable	105 dr.
Total receipts in this term	1,982 dr., 5 ob.

Statement of money received in the archonship of Archon

(nothing entered)

Statement of expenditures during the autumn term (346 B.C.) in the archonship of Damoxenos, when the Amphictyony was headed by Kottyphos and Kolosimmos.

laurel	1 ½ ob.
reed pen	4 ½ ob.

pay for guarding the flock	1 1/2 ob.
pay for the cooks of the victims	3 dr. 2 ob.
Total expenses during the autumn	4 dr., 3 ½ ob.

Statement of expenditures during the spring term (345 B.C.) in the archonship of Damoxenos.

To Praxion and Aristandros of Tegea, who contracted to transport 40 crossbeams for the colonnade from the sea to the sanctuary, one-tenth of the contract was held back, and we paid	1,306 dr.
To Nikodemos of Argos, a stone-cutter, for cutting six crossbeams from Corinth, holding back a tenth we paid	245 dr.
To Xenodoros, the architect, salary for half a year	210 dr.
The cost of a box to store writing tablets	22 dr., 5 ob.
Repair of a box	1 dr., 3 ob.
Laurel	2 ob.
Pay for the cooks of the victims	3 dr., 2 ob.
Writing tablet	1 ¼ ob.
Pay for a secretary	40 dr.
Pay for a herald	2 dr.
To Teledamos of Delphi for three benches on which the naopoioi sit	9 dr.
To Eukrates of Delphi for the stele on which the names of the naopoioi are inscribed	5 dr., 3 ob.
Total expenses for this term (spring 345)	1845 dr., 4 ½ ob.

[This section, which is largely mutilated, contained the accounts for the autumn of 345 B.C. It concludes with:]

For transport of a file-box	1 ob.
Total expenses for this term	199 dr. 3 ob.

Expenditures during the spring term (344 B.C.) in the archonship of Archon.

For the drainage of water around the temple	1 ½ ob.
Laurel	1 ob.
Pay for guarding the flock	3 ob.
Pay for the cooks of the victims	3 dr., 2 ob.
Pay for a herald	2 dr.
Half a year's salary for the architect Xenodoros	360 dr.
Pay for a secretary	40 dr.
Total expenses for this term	406 dr., 1 ½ ob.

Statement of expenditures in the autumn term (344 B.C.) in the the archonship of Thebagoras.

Two days' worth of laurel	2 1/3 ob.
For guarding the flock	4 ½ ob.
Cost of a reed-pen	1 dr.
Pay for the cooks of the victims	3 dr., 2 ob.
To Eukrates for smoothing a stele on which are the names of the naopoioi	2 dr.
To Eukrates for moving the bases and the statues of Onomarchos and Philomelos out of the sanctuary	8 dr., 3 ob.
To Kleon for removing the statues of the horses and the other statues and for draining water around the sanctuary	7 dr.
To Athanogeiton the Boeotian for cleaning the stones near the temple	20 dr.
Pay for a herald	2 dr.
To Xenodoros the architect, half a year's salary	360 dr.
Pay for a secretary	40 dr.
Athanogeiton the Boeotian received the contract for cutting Corinthian marble to replace destroyed stones: 6 architraves, 14 triglyphs, and 7 cornices. The contract is for 1,036 dr. Holding back a tenth, we paid	931 dr.

Agathonymos the Corinthian received the
contract for transporting stone from Lechaion
to Kirrha . . .

[The rest is lost.]

69. SPEUSIPPOS' LETTER TO PHILIP, CA. 343 B.C.
Translation based on E. Bickermann and J. Sykutris' text in *Speusipps Brief an König Philipp*, Leipzig, 1928, pp. 7-12

Speusippos was a nephew of Plato. He became head of the Academy after Plato's death in 347 B.C. The career of Philip of Macedon furnished rich material for contemporary propagandists. The following letter is an interesting example of the efforts which were made to enhance Philip's image. Speusippos commends Antipatros to Philip for historical research that bears closely on Philip's situation. The letter takes the form of an extended criticism of the *Address to Philip* (oration No. 5) by Isocrates, published in 346 B.C. Rivalry between the schools of Isocrates and Plato produced this type of personal invective. For other similar documents concerning Philip, see Isocrates' *Address to Philip* (available abridged in W. R. Connor *Greek Orations*, Ann Arbor, 1967) and *The Letter of Philip* (Pseudo-Demosthenes 12, also in *Greek Orations*) in which Philip defends himself against charges of barbarity and dishonesty. For these charges, see Demosthenes' *Olynthiac* and *Philippic Orations*.

Speusippos to King Philip, Greetings.
Antipatros, the bearer of this letter, is a Magnesian (i.e. from Thessaly) who has spent a long time in Athens writing on Greek history. He says that he is being illtreated by someone in Magnesia. Would you listen to his problem and help him as much as you can? He deserves your aid for many reasons, including the following incident. In a class he read to us the speech which Isocrates had sent to you (i.e., the *Address to Philip*). He praised its basic structure, but criticized it for omitting many of the benefits which you have done for Greece. I will try to describe some of them, because Isocrates has neither revealed the favors which you and your ancestors have done for Greece, nor dispelled the slanders

which some make against you, nor refrained from attacking Plato in the speeches he has sent you.

In the first place, Isocrates should not have been silent about your close ties with our city (Athens), but should have made it plain also for your posterity. For when Herakles wished to be initiated (into the Mysteries of Eleusis), and there was a law forbidding initiation to non-citizens, he became the adoptive son of Pylios. Therefore it was possible for Isocrates to have addressed you as a fellow citizen, since your family is descended from Herakles. Next he could have mentioned the good deeds your ancestor Alexander and your other ancestors did for Greece (see Herodotos 5.18-20; 7.172-173; 9.44). For when Xerxes sent envoys to Greece demanding earth and water (the tokens of submission), Alexander slew them. And later, when the barbarians were on the march and the Greeks met them near your sanctuary of Herakles, Alexander warned the Greeks of the treachery of Aleuas and the Thessalians so that the Greeks withdrew and were saved. These matters deserved mention not by Herodotos and Damastes only, but by Isocrates as well in his speeches (*Address to Philip* 77) . . . [The text is corrupt here] . . . win favor towards you from the hearers. He ought to have told the incident at Plataia during Mardonios' campaign, and the rest of the series of benefits your ancestors did. Thus, his speech about you would have gained you goodwill among the Greeks. As it was, he said nothing good about your kingdom. Ancient history would have been fitting for Isocrates to relate, ancient as he himself is, and the artful drafting of prize orations is something, as he himself says (*Address to Philip* 10), best left to a young talent.

It was no less part of his task to destroy the slanders against you, most of which are spread by the Olynthians. For why should people believe that you, involved in war against Illyria, Thrace, Athens, Sparta and other Greeks and barbarians, would have been so foolish as to begin war with Olynthos? This letter is not the place to go into detail; but I will describe something which ought to be publicized, although no one talks about it. It will, however, be advantageous for you to know this and I think you will agree that Antipatros deserves a reward for announcing it. The bearer of this letter is the first and only person to have convincingly demonstrated that the land which belonged to the Olynthians was originally the property of the descendants of Herakles and not of the Greeks in Chalcidice. For Herakles destroyed Neleus in Messene and Syleus near Amphipolis because they were dangers to other peoples. He gave Messene to Nestor the son of Neleus and Phyllis (i.e. the region of Amphipolis) to Dikaios the brother of Syleus, but only for safe keeping. Many generations later, Kresphontes siezed Messene and the Athenians and Chalcidians seized the territory of Amphipolis, although it was all Heraklid property. In similar fashion Herakles destroyed other malefactors and criminals, Hippokoon the tyrant in Sparta and Alkyoneus in Pallene. He entrusted Sparta to Tyndareus and Poteidaia with the rest of Pallene to Sithon the son of Poseidon. Laconia was taken by the sons of Aristodemos during the Return of the Herakleidai, but Pallene was occupied by Eretrians and Corinthians and Achaians returning from Troy, even though it too was Heraklid property. Antipatros has also discovered that, in like manner, Herakles killed Tmolos and Telegonos, the Protid tyrants in Torone, and slew Kleidas and his sons in Ambrakia; Torone he gave for safe-keeping to Aristomachos the son of Sithon, but the Chalcidians occupied it although it was your land. He entrusted Ambrakia to Ladikes and Charattes, intending that all these deposits should be ultimately delivered to his descendants. Furthermore, all Macedonians know about the more recent settlements of Alexander in the Edonian land. All this material consists of sound arguments which can help your power, unlike the sophistries and empty rhetoric of Isocrates.

Because it is plain that you are presently involved deeply in the affairs of the (Delphic) Amphictyony, I want to tell you a story which I got from Antipatros, how the Amphictyony was first set up, and how Amphictyonic states were destroyed, the Phlegyai by Apollo, the Dryopes by Herakles, and the Kirrhaians by the other Amphictyons. All these had been Amphictyons, and their seats were taken away from them and given to other nations. Antipatros says that you have emulated these ancient proceedings by means of your campaign to Delphi and getting as your prize the two votes of the Phokians. But the man (Isocrates) who claims to "tell ancient deeds in modern fashion and recent deeds in archaic fashion" (Isocrates, *Panegyrikos* 8) has told neither the ancient events nor the recent deeds done by you nor the events in between. Indeed, he seems to have never heard of the first, never seen the second, and forgotten all the rest.

Isocrates, our orator, by way of spurring you on to just deeds, has exhibited the exile and return of Alkibiades as an example (*Address to Philip* 58-61), but the greater and fairer deeds of your father he has completely omitted. For Alkibiades was exiled for impiety and returned to his country after doing damage to her. Your father, on the other hand, overcome by his rivals, retreated for a short time and then recaptured control of Macedon. Alkibiades was exiled for a second time and ended his life in disgrace; Amyntas grew old on his throne. Isocrates also offers you the case of the monarchy of Dionysios (*Address to Philip* 65), as if you were supposed to imitate the worst instead of the best. And he says (*Address to Philip* 113) that examples should be familiar or close to home, but then, spurning his own advice, proceeds to employ the most grotesque, irrelevant and contradictory examples imaginable. The absurdest part of the whole speech comes when he declares that his ridiculous arguments have served to eliminate the criticisms which his pupils made of the earlier drafts (*Address to Philip* 22); the truth is that his pupils are his intellectual slaves and chattel, so that they have ranked his letter to you as his all-time masterpiece (*Address to Philip* 23). You may easily judge for yourself Isocrates' erudition and historical wisdom when you hear that he calls Cyrene a colony of Sparta (*Address to Philip* 5), although everyone else knows it was settled by Thera; he also designates his pupil from the Black Sea as the true heir to his wisdom. You have seen many charlatans in your position, but I assure you, none more disgusting than that pupil.

I learn that Theopompos (pupil of Isocrates and an historian) is with you, that blood-chilling character, and that he is slandering Plato. As if Plato had not been instrumental in establishing your kingdom in the reign of Perdikkas and was not continually vexed by any appearance of fraternal strife. In order to put a stop to the nasty beast, merely direct Antipatros to recite a portion of his *Greek History* to him. Theopompos will learn that his just fate is the eraser, and that he need expect no support from you.

And Isocrates — when he was a young man he and Timotheos wrote scurrilous memoranda to the Assembly against your people. Now that he is old, he still appears to hate or envy all your good qualities, so that he does not mention them. Instead he has sent you a speech which he first wrote for Agesilaus; revising it a little, he peddled it to Dionysios the tyrant of Syracuse; next, making a few additions and subtractions, he used it to court Alexander the Thessalian; finally he has discharged it, somewhat shopworn by this time, in your direction. I could wish there were room on this letter-form to discuss all the cheap tricks he plays in the speech as you received it. In regard to Amphipolis (*Address to Philip* 7), he says that the conclusion of peace prevents him from writing a speech on the problem; about the immortality of Herakles (*Address to Philip* 33), he says he will discourse for you "some other time;" at some points he begs for forgiveness for sloppy writing caused by old age (*Address to Philip* 149); do not, he says, be surprised if his messenger from the Black Sea recites the speech so as to make it seem worse than it really is (*Address to Philip* 26ff.); as to how Persia may be defeated, that, he says, is a thing you yourself know best (*Address to Philip* 105). But I have not sufficient paper to list the rest of his excuses. Since the Persian King captured Egypt we have had a scarcity.

Good health to you; send Antipatros back to us when you have taken care of his needs.

70. PHOKIS PAYS REPARATIONS FOR THE SACRED WAR, 342 B.C.
Tod 172, abridged

Abandoned by Athens and pressed by Philip and Thebes, the Phokians abandoned Delphi and surrendered in 346 B.C. (see No. 67). Phokis suffered the following penalties: the country was disarmed, its cities were dissolved into villages, and it was required to repay the money stolen from Apollo, a sum reckoned as 10,000 talents. The debt was to be repaid at the rate of thirty talents semiannually. The following inscription records the second installment, spring 342 B.C. The ending of the Sacred War also altered the composition of the Amphictyony. The earlier representation had been as follows:

        Thessalians
        Boeotians
        Dorians

Ionians (Athens held these seats)
Perrhaibians
Dolopes
Magnesians
Lokrians
Ainianians (sometimes listed as Oitaians)
Phthiotians (sometimes Achaians)
Malians
Phokians

The representation after 346 B.C. is shown by the list of representatives (*hieromnemones*) given in the inscription. The Phokians have been completely expelled and were replaced by the Delphians (see No. 68); the Perrhaibians and Dolopians have been combined, and Philip has become a tribe. He now had an important role in a shrine sacred to all of Greece. He had acquired a presence in Central Greece that would give him the opportunity for further intervention: No. 72.

When the following were in office at the spring session, the Phokians repaid thirty talents as the second installment of their debt to the sanctuary. In the archonship of Kleon, when the following men were *prytaneis*: Echetimos, Herakleides, Antagoras, Ariston, Philinos, Choirikos, Aneritos, and Sodamos. The following were *hieromnemones*:

Kottyphos and Kolosimmos	Thessalians
Eurylochos and Kleandros	Philip
Damon and Mnasidamos	Delphians
Nikon of Matropolis and Deinomenes of Argos	Dorians
Timondas and Mnesilochos of Athens	Ionians
Phaikos and Asandros	Perrhaibians and Dolopes
Daitadas and Olympion	Boeotians
Pleisteas and Theomnastos	Lokrians
Agasikratos and Pythodoros	Achaians
Philonautas and Epikratidas	Magnesians
Agelaos and Kleomenes	Ainianians
Antimachos of Herakleia in Trachis and Demokrates of Lamia	Malians

71. ATHENS GRANTS PRIVILEGES TO ARYBBAS THE MOLOSSIAN, CA. 342 B.C.
Tod 173

Arybbas was a son of Alketas, king of the Molossian tribe in Epirus. Alketas was a member of the Second Athenian Confederacy (No. 22). When Alketas died, Arybbas shared the throne with his brother Neoptolemos, and then ruled alone after his brother's death. Neoptolemos was the father of Olympias, who married Philip II of Macedon and was the mother of Alexander III the Great. In 343/2 B.C. Philip expelled Arybbas and replaced him with Olympias' brother (named Alexander). Arybbas fled to Athens and invoked the grant of citizenship made to his father. Athens passed a favorable decree, which also resolved to restore him to his kingdom. Athens, after the Peace of Philokrates, was again in a state of war with Philip. The bottom of the stone is a relief of a victorious charioteer, illustrating the victories named in the inscription.

Gods. In honor of Arybbas.... The right of citizenship and the other gifts given to his father and grandfather are all to be given to him and his descendants. Arybbas is to be cared for and protected from harm. The Council and the generals, now and for all time, should always protect him, and also should every citizen of Athens. He will always have access to the Council and the Assembly whenever he wishes. Those who are in prytany at any time should see to it that he is granted such access. The secretary of the Council will inscribe this decree on a stone stele and erect it on the Acropolis. The Treasurer of the People will give thirty drachmas for the inscribing out of the money budgeted for decrees. Let Arybbas be invited to dine at the Prytaneion tomorrow, and let those who are with him also be invited to dine at the Prytaneion tomorrow. Let there also be consideration about the other matters raised by Arybbas. Let the resolution of the Council be approved, but add to it the following: if anyone slays with violent death Arybbas or any of his children, he will suffer the same penalty as he would for killing any other Athenian. The generals now and future will see to it that Arybbas and his children recover his ancestral kingdom.

(Below are three crowns, with titles as below, and then the relief described in the commentary:)

At Olympia	At Delphi	At Olympia
victor	victor	...

72. ATHENS GRANTS HONORS TO TENEDOS, 339 B.C.
Tod 175

Philip took complete control of Thrace in 342 B.C., finally deposing Kersebleptes. Athens saw this as a threat to the vital Chersonese and, at Demosthenes' urging, broke the Peace of Philokrates (see No. 70). Byzantium and Perinthos were also alarmed, left their alliance with Philip, and received aid from Athens when he attacked them. The following decree voices Athens' gratitude to the island of Tenedos, which perhaps figured in these operations against Philip. Tenedos had always been a loyal ally to Athens. Near the end of the inscription Athens takes the opportunity to rebuke those who complained about the Confederacy.

In the archonship of Theophrastos (340/39), the Assembly passed the following decree. Kekropis held the eighth prytany (ca. April), Aspetos son of Demostratos from Kytherros was the secretary, and Kallikrates son of Charopides from Lamptrai made the motion: concerning what the people of Tenedos said, the people of Tenedos are to be publicly praised because of their virtue and good will toward the people of Athens and her allies which has been shown in the past and was shown now again. So that the people of Tenedos may receive the money which they are owed by the people of Athens, during Theophrastos' archonship (340/39) (they are to be repaid).... These are to be the conditions for repayment until they have received back all their money. During this time there is to be no levy either by a general or by anyone else, either in silver or in any other metal, nor is there to be any new taxation imposed during this time by the *synhedrion* of the Confederacy, until the people of Tenedos receive all the money which they have lent, so that for all time everyone may know, whether they be allies or anyone else friendly to the people of Athens, that the people of Athens care rightly about those of their allies who benefit the people of Athens and her allies. The people of Tenedos are to be publicly praised and crowned with a gold crown valued at 1,000 drachmas because of their virtue and good will towards the people of Athens and their allies. The Tenedian *synhedros*, Aratos, is to be publicly commended and crowned with a wreath of olive. The other Tenedian *synhedroi* are also to be publicly commended.

[The end is lost.]

73. BATTLE OF CHAIRONEIA, 338 B.C.
Tod 176

Fourth century Greek history to 338 B.C. is a continuation of the struggle for the hegemony of Greece which began in the fifth century. The most important battles of the fourth century were Knidos (No. 10), Naxos (No. 25), Leuctra (No. 33), where Sparta lost control of her empire, Mantineia (No. 47), where Thebes lost her preeminent position in Greece, and Chaironeia in 338 B.C., where Macedon ended the Greek city-states' struggles for hegemony and established its monarchy as the ruling power of the Greeks.

The following poem, preserved only partly on stone, but preserved completely in the Palatine Anthology (7.245), commemorates the Athenian dead at the battle of Chaironeia. Its author is unknown.

Faced with a rebuff at Byzantium (see No. 72), Philip decided to carry the war to Athens by land. He had the opportunity provided for him. In 339 B.C. the city state of Amphissa at Theban instigation brought a charge of sacrilege against Athens. Aeschines, the Athenian orator, happened to be at the Amphictyonic meeting. By a brilliant maneuver he cleared Athens of the charge and instead instigated a motion of war against Amphissa. Demosthenes, whose own policy was one of close co-operation with Thebes, persuaded the Athenian Assembly not to join in this Sacred War on Amphissa. Thebes, with her own anti-Athenian party now discredited by the failure of the plan to crush Athens, also refused to join the war. The League, without the co-operation of both Athens and Thebes, voted to call in Philip to prosecute the war. Philip, technically an ally of Thebes, invited the Thebans to join him in the expedition. The Athenians, won over by Demosthenes, allied on terms very favorable to the Thebans who were now convinced of the danger Philip represented to the freedom of the Greeks. The Thebans refused to allow Philip passage to central Greece. With great military brilliance Philip created a situation at Chaironeia in which the Athenians broke their battle line formation and the Macedonian left wing under Alexander rolled up the Thebans on the Greeks' right wing. Macedon became the hegemon of the Greeks (see No. 74).

> Time, surveyor of all human activity,
> Announce our deeds to the rest of mankind.
> We died in the fields of Boeotia,
> Dying to save the holy land, Hellas.

74. PEACE OF 338/7 B.C.
Tod 177

After the battle of Chaironeia Philip called representatives of all the states of Greece to a meeting at Corinth. Only Sparta refused to come. At this meeting a new League was founded, comprising all the Greek states who were to be represented in a *synhedrion*. A leader was to be chosen to direct the League and implement the *synhedrion's* decrees. The leader was obviously to be Philip. As the oath in this inscription indicates, the Corinthian League would settle any trouble between its members and would not allow any revolutionary activity. Macedonian garrisons were to be stationed at strategic points, and the size of a city's representation in the *synhedrion* depended on its contribution in arms and men to the League's army. Philip forged violently the unity of the Greeks by the same basic means the other Greek states had tried: garrisons, governors and tribute.

One of the avowed purposes of the League was to free all the Greeks, because the Greeks of Asia Minor were still under the control of the Persian King or his satraps. Thus, the old dream of repaying the Persians for their invasions of 490 and 480 B.C., and for meddling in the affairs of the Greeks (No. 15) was resurrected. The League formed the "legal" basis for Philip's and Alexander's invasion of Persia. Death cut short Philip's role as hegemon, but Alexander reaffirmed the League on his accession and used it to levy Greek troops for his own invasion of Persia. The Macedonian garrisons and governors installed by Philip kept the Greek city states loyal while Alexander conquered Persia.

I swear by Zeus, Earth, Sun, Poseidon, Athena, Ares, and all the gods and goddesses that I will keep the Peace, and I will not break the treaties with Philip of Macedon. I will not bear arms with hostile intent by land or by sea against those who keep the oaths, nor will I attack in war by any device or stratagem any city, fort, or harbor which belongs to anyone who shares in the Peace. I will not oppose the kingship of Philip and his offspring nor those constitutions that were in effect in each city when it swore the oath of peace. I will not do anything against the oath, and will prevent anyone else from doing so as far as I can. If anyone does anything against the oath, I will aid in so far as possible those who have been wronged in the way they want me to. I will fight whoever transgresses the common peace in so far as it seems best to the common council and the leader's orders. I will not abandon . . .

[The end is lost.]

75. ATHENIAN LAW AGAINST TYRANNY, 336 B.C.
Hesperia XXI, 1952, p. 355

The restoration of the Athenian democracy in 403 B.C. was decisive. Strife between oligarchs and democrats, a lively issue in fifth century Athens, did not exist in the fourth century. Not only was there no internal threat to the democracy, but also no major changes were made in its structure. Philip's conquest of Greece created widespread fear that Macedon might employ subversion and revolution as an instrument of control. The peace treaties made between the Greeks and Philip, and later Alexander, contained assurances against this (see No. 74 and also pseudo-Demosthenes 17, which concerns the treaty with Alexander). Similar provisions are found in Nos. 46 and 49. The following law publicizes Athens' determination to discourage attempts to destroy the democracy. The date of the decree is very close to that of the assassination of Philip and the accession of Alexander. The stone (see Plate p. 108) is in perfect condition. The relief at the top depicts Democracy crowning the people of Athens.

In the archonship of Phrynichos (337/6), when Leontis held the ninth prytany (ca. June 336), and Chairestratos son of Ameinias from Acharne was secretary, the *proedros* Menestratos from Aixone put the vote, and Eukrates son of Aristotimos from Peiraieus had made the motion: with good fortune for the people of Athens, be it decreed by the *nomothetai* that if anyone attacks the Athenian people with the intent of establishing a tyranny or collaborates in establishing a tyranny or destroys the democracy at Athens or its assembly, anyone who slays the doer of such deeds will be sacrosanct. And if the Assembly and democracy of Athens are overthrown, no member of the Council of the Areopagos will go up on to the Areopagos, serve in that Council or be involved in any of its business. If the Assembly or democracy of Athens is overthrown, and any member of the Council of the Areopagos goes up on to the Areopagos or serves in that Council or is involved in any of its business, he will be disenfranchised, both himself and his posterity, and his property will be confiscated, and a tithe will go to the goddess. Let the secretary of the Council inscribe this law on two stone stelai and erect one copy at the entrance to the Areopagos before the Council-house and the other in the Assembly. Let the treasurer of the Assembly disburse twenty drachmas for the inscribing of the stelai from the funds budgeted for such purposes.

Plate IV Democracy crowning the people of Athens, 336 B.C. (Courtesy of the American School of Classical Studies at Athens)

76. SICILIAN TREATIES, 405-339 B.C.

After the defeat of the Sicilian expedition in 413 B.C., Syracuse moved towards empire. No other Sicilian city could withstand her. Segesta, however, the city of the Elymi, which had originally called in Athens in the dispute over territory with Selinous, now called on Carthage as champion. The Carthaginians, who controlled the western portion of the island with their headquarters at Lilybaion (modern Marsala), complied. Carthage took and sacked Selinous, Himera and Akragas and by 405 B.C. threatened Syracuse. Under these circumstances Dionysios seized control of Syracuse, became tyrant and galvanized resistance against the Carthaginians. Dionysios' efforts gained him the rule of Syracuse and Sicily until his death in 367 B.C. As such he was courted by the powers of Greece (see Nos. 11 and 38) and also by the Athenian philosopher Plato (see Plato's *Seventh Letter*).

The four following treaties show the struggle between Greek and Carthaginian for Sicily. In the first treaty *A*, shortly after Dionysios' seizure of Syracuse, Carthage controlled almost the entire island. In the second treaty *B* Dionysios had recovered almost all of the island, as the Carthaginians probably maintained control only of Panormos, Lilybaeum and the territory of the Elymi and Sikans. Dionysios at this time also began his successful bid to build an empire in southern Italy and Molossia. In the third treaty *C* the Carthaginians had rewon part of the central territory of Sicily and the dividing line mentioned in this treaty, the Halykos river, remained the frontier between Greek and Carthaginian until the First Punic War (264-241 B.C.).

In the fourth treaty *D* the river Halykos is once again reaffirmed as the frontier between Greek and Carthaginian. After Dionysios I's reign his son, Dionysios II (367-345 B.C.), succeeded to the tyranny. He could not, however, control his father's empire. Disgruntled citizens called on a Corinthian general, Timoleon, to lead them against the tyrant. Timoleon was extremely successful, expelling Dionysios II in 345 B.C. and, afterwards, other tyrants who had installed themselves during the dissolution of the Syracusan empire. Timoleon was also successful against the Carthaginian encroachments on Greek territory as the Carthaginians tried to capitalize on the internal conflicts of the Greeks.

A. Bengtson 210 = Diodorus Siculus 13.114.1, 405 B.C.

The Carthaginians will hold the Elymi and Sikans, the original inhabitants (of the west of the island); the citizens of Selinous, Akragas and Himera as well as those of Gela and Camarina are to be allowed to dwell in their cities and will pay tribute to Carthage; the citizens of Leontinoi and Messana and the Sikels will all be autonomous; the Syracusans will be subject to Dionysios; captives and ships are to be returned to their original allegiance.

B. Bengtson 233 = Diodorus Siculus 14.96.4, 392 B.C.

The conditions (of the peace treaty) were similar to the previous peace treaty (see above), except that the Sikels were now to be subject to Dionysios and that he was to take possession of Tauromenion.

C. Bengtson 261 = Diodorus Siculus 15.17.5, 376 or 374 B.C.

... Peace was declared on the terms that both should keep what they had. There were, however, two exceptions. The Carthaginians were to hold Selinous and its territory and also Akragas as far as the river Halykos. Dionysios was to pay the Carthaginians one thousand talents.

D. Bengtson 344 = Diodorus Siculus 16.82.3, 339 B.C.

... All the Greek cities are to be free; the river Halykos is to be the boundary of the Carthaginian and Syracusan territory; and the Carthaginians are not to aid the tyrants who are at war with Syracuse.

GLOSSARY

acropolis: the citadel of a Greek city. In Athens it was the center of the civic religion, containing such buildings as the Erechtheion and the Parthenon. In the documents, many decrees are to be erected on the Acropolis.

agora: in Athens, the area northwest of the Acropolis, marked off as the center of public business. On its square were buildings which housed the offices of the chief officials, such as the *bouleuterion* for the Council, the prytaneion, the offices of the archons, and the law courts. The market area which lay nearby was also called the agora, but it is the civic center which is meant in the documents.

apodektai: a board of ten officials, who supervised the receipt of state income and its distribution to the various offices for spending.

archons: the nine chief magistrates of Athens: the *eponymous archon* (after whom the year was named, and whose name appears as a date at the head of decrees); the *king-archon*; the *polemarch*; and six *thesmothetai*. After 487 B.C. they were chosen by lot. Their duties were mainly judicial. The title is common in Greek states, as for example the Thessalian League in No. 49.

Assembly: the meeting of Athenian citizens which, acting in concert with the Council, held sovereign control of state affairs. Its meetings took place at the Pnyx, southwest of the Acropolis. Four meetings a month were required by law.

astynomoi: officials mentioned in No. 61, apparently in charge of market and trade regulations.

Athena Promachos: the giant statue of Athena the Champion, located prominently on the Acropolis.

Boeotarchs: the chief military commanders of the Boeotian League. Epameinondas and Pelopidas were prominent Boeotarchs of the fourth century (see Nos. 33, 36, 42, and 46). Their position in the Boeotian constitution in 395 B.C. is described in No. 3, chapter XVI, when their number was eleven. Nos. 35 and 42 give lists of the Boeotarchs at the later period (after 371) when they were seven.

Council (*Boulē*): in Athens, the body of 500 citizens which prepared business for the Assembly and acted as its executive. Decrees describe themselves as joint productions of both bodies. The Council was made up of fifty men from each tribe, and each tribal group presided over the Council for one-tenth of the year in rotation.

decarchy: the form of pro-Spartan oligarchy which Lysander installed in the cities of the Athenian empire after the Peloponnesian War: usually consisting of ten men, but the Thirty at Athens are a good example (see No. 1).

deme: a local township of Attica. There were over 170 of them, and membership in one was the basis of Athenian citizenship. In the documents, an Athenian citizen is commonly identified by 1) his own name 2) his father's name 3) his deme; e.g., in No. 23, Aristoteles son of Euphiletos from Acharne.

drachma: the normal unit of money (see Table p. 115). An Athenian drachma was a silver coin weighing about one-sixth of an ounce.

Eleven: the board of public officials at Athens who were in charge of the imprisonment and execution of criminals. Those who had held this office under the Thirty were excluded from the amnesty which followed the restoration of the democracy in 403 B.C.

Ephors: the chief magistrates of Sparta. Five in number, they possessed wide powers, including powers to arrest the kings and preside over the assembly.

generals (*strategoi*): the supreme military commanders of Athens. Ten in number, and elected annually.

harmost: title of the governors sent by Sparta to rule cities of her empire, or cities occupied by Spartan forces.

Helots: inhabitants of Laconia and Messenia kept by Sparta in a servile status. The enslavement of Messenia freed the Spartans from the necessity of agricultural labor and permitted them to devote themselves entirely to military training. The liberation of Messenia by Epameinondas in 379 permanently crippled Sparta.

hipparchs: the two supreme commanders of Athens' cavalry, elected annually.

metic: holder of the highest non-citizen status in a Greek state.

mina: unit of money (see Table p. 115) equal to 100 drachmas. Also a unit of weight (approximately one pound), as probably in No. 61.

Mysteries: the great festival of Demeter and Persephone, held at Eleusis under the direction of Athens each Boedromion. (Referred to in No. 2.)

nomothetai: a lawcourt, charged with the task of ratifying proposed changes in the law of Athens. (Referred to in No. 75.)

obol: a coin equal to one-sixth of a drachma (see Table p. 115).

Panathenaia: the festival held in honor of Athens and her chief tutelary Athena each year in Hekatombaion, and with especial grandeur in every fourth year. Highlighted by a parade which proceeded through the agora and terminated in the Parthenon. The festival was often

employed as a suitable occasion for allies to demonstrate their loyalty to Athens (see No. 31).
proedroi: the nine men allotted to preside over a session of the Athenian Assembly. They were chosen by the *epistates* of the *prytaneis* (who omitted his own tribe); the nine chosen then chose one of themselves to be chairman of the meeting.
prostatai: officials of Ioulis, mentioned in No. 61, charged with prosecuting violations of the ocher-regulations.
proxenos: one who was recognized by his own state as having a relation of friendship with another Greek state. Such a person would be expected to take a special interest in the affairs of his home state insofar as they affected the other one. He would, for example, provide hospitality for its ambassadors. In No. 60 the Boeotian *proxenos* in Tenedos may have acted as agent for Tenedians who supported Thebes in the Third Sacred War.
prytany: The Council of Athens was made of fifty men from each tribe. The year was divided into ten parts, called prytanies, in each of which the men from one tribe supervised the affairs of the Council. The fifty were called *prytaneis* for this period. One man, called the *epistates*, was allotted to serve as chairman over his fellow prytaneis each day. *Prytanis* is also the title of the eponymous magistrates of Mytilene and Phokaia in No. 13.
prytaneion: the circular building in the agora which served as office-space for the prytaneis (see **prytany**). Mentioned in the documents as the site for state banquets held for ambassadors or persons receiving public honors.
prytanis/prytaneis: see prytany.
satrap: provincial governor of the Persian Empire, holding his territory in fee from the Emperor.
stele: a slab of stone on which items such as, e.g., public documents were inscribed, set up free-standing. Illustrated in Plates I, II, and IV.
stele of the allies: Document No. 22, so called in Nos. 21 and 25.
synhedrion: see
synhedroi: the representatives from the members of the Second Athenian Confederacy. They formed an assembly called the *synhedrion*, whose vote on Confederacy matters was equal to that of Athens. No. 31 contains a decree of the *synhedrion*.
talent: a unit of money (see Table p. 115), equal to 6000 drachmas. Also a unit of weight (about sixty pounds), as probably in No. 61.
taxiarch: in Athens, the commander of the infantry from a single tribe.
Thirty: the oligarchy imposed on Athens after the Peloponnesian War. See *decarchy*, and No. 1.
tribe: the citizens of Athens were divided into ten tribes (see Table p. 115), and Athenian government was based upon this division. The prytany of the Council, for example, rotated from tribe to tribe throughout the year, and the army was brigaded by tribal contingents.

TABLES

1. Athenian Eponymous Archons, 403-336 B.C.

403/2	Eukleides	376/5	Charisandros
402/1	Mikon	375/4	Hippodamas
401/0	Xenainetos	374/3	Sokratides
400/399	Laches	373/2	Asteios
399/8	Aristokrates	372/1	Alkisthenes
398/7	Euthykles	371/0	Phrasikleides
397/6	Souniades	370/69	Dysniketos
396/5	Phormion	369/8	Lysistratos
395/4	Diophantos	368/7	Nausigenes
394/3	Euboulides	367/6	Polyzelos
393/2	Demostratos	366/5	Kephisodoros
392/1	Philokles	365/4	Chion
391/0	Nikoteles	364/3	Timokrates
390/89	Demostratos	363/2	Charikleides
389/8	Antipatros	362/1	Molon
388/7	Pyrgion	361/0	Nikophemos
387/6	Theodotos	360/59	Kallimedes
386/5	Mystichides	359/8	Eucharistos
385/4	Dexitheos	358/7	Kephisodotos
384/3	Dieitrephes	357/6	Agathokles
383/2	Phanostratos	356/5	Elpines
382/1	Euandros	355/4	Kallistratos
381/0	Demophilos	354/3	Diotimos
380/79	Pytheas	353/2	Thoudemos
379/8	Nikon	352/1	Aristodemos
378/7	Nausinikos	351/0	Theellos
377/6	Kalleas	350/49	Apollodoros

349/8	Kallimachos	342/1	Sosigenes
348/7	Theophilos	341/0	Nikomachos
347/6	Themistokles	340/39	Theophrastos
346/5	Archias	339/8	Lysimachides
345/4	Euboulos	338/7	Chairondas
344/3	Lysiskos	337/6	Phrynichos
343/2	Pythodotos	336/5	Pythodelos

2. The ten Athenian Tribes in their official order

Erechtheis	Oineis
Aigeis	Kekropis
Pandionis	Hippothontis
Leontis	Aiantis
Akamantis	Antiochis

3. The twelve Athenian Months

Hekatombaion	Maimakterion	Elaphebolion
Metageitnion	Posideion	Mounychion
Boedromion	Gamelion	Thargelion
Pyanepsion	Anthesterion	Skirophorion

The Athenian year began near the summer solstice, around June 21. Hence, an archon's year in office is designated by two years, e.g., Eukleides' year as archon = 403/2 B.C. = ca. June 21 of 403 B.C. to June 20 of 402 B.C.

4. Athenian Money Standards

6 obols = 1 drachma
100 drachmas = 1 mina
60 minas = 1 talent

Aeginetan Money Standards

6 obols = 1 drachma   35 staters = 1 mina
2 drachmas = 1 stater   60 minas = 1 talent

When converting Athenian money to Aeginetan money the following exchange rate was used:

7 Aeginetan drachmas = 10 Athenian drachmas
2 Aeginetan drachmas = 3 Athenian drachmas

5. Spartan Kings

Agiads
    Pausanias 409-395
    Agesipolis I 395-380
    Kleombrotos I 380-371
    Agesipolis II 371-370
    Kleomenes II 370-309

Eurypontids
    Agis II 427-399
    Agesilaus II 399-360
    Archidamos III 360-338
    Agis III 338-331

6. Persian Emperors

Artaxerxes II Mnemon 404-359
Artaxerxes III Ochos 359-338
Arses 338-336
Darius III Codomannus 336-331

7. Macedonian Kings

Archelaos 413-399
Orestes 399-396
Aeropus 396-393
Amyntas II and Pausanias 393-392
Amyntas III 393-370
Alexander II 370-369/8
Ptolemy 369/8-365
Perdikkas III 365-359
Philip II 359-336
Alexander III 336-323

8. Concordance of Sources

W/V	Tod, GHI	SIG^3	IG	Bengtson	Other
1	97	117	ii^2 1		
2				213	
3					P. Oxy. 842
4					Xen. Hell. 3.5.8-15
5	101	122	ii^2 14	223	
6	102		ii^2 15	224	
7	103	123	ii^2 16	229	
8	104	131	ii^2 5222		
9	105	130	ii^2 6217		
10	107	124 & 125	ii^2 1656 & 1657		
11	108	128	ii^2 18		
12	111	135		231	
13	112		xii (2).1	228	
14	113	134			
15				242	

117

W/V	Tod, GHI	SIG³	IG	Bengtson	Other
16	116	137	ii² 29		
17	118	142	ii² 34 & 35	248	
18	120		v(1) 1565		
19	121	146	ii² 41	256	
20	122	149	ii² 42	258	
21			ii² 40	255	
22	123	147	ii² 43	257	
23	124	148	ii² 44	259	
24	125	153	ii² 1635		
25	126	150	ii² 96	262	
26	127	151	ii² 97	263	
27					Xen. *Hell.* 6.1.4-16
28				265	
29	129	157	ii² 102	264	
30			ii² 1609 vv. 83-110		
31					Accame, *Lega Ateniese* p. 230
32				269	
33	130		vii 2462		
34				270	
35		179	vii 2407		
36					*Wiener Jahreshefte* 33 (1941) p. 38
37	135	165	ii² 106		
38	136	163	ii² 105 & 523	280	
39	137				
40	138	167			
41					*Athenische Mitteilungen* 51 (1926) p. 36
42			vii 2408		
43	140	239b			
44	142	173	ii² 111	289	
45	143	174	ii² 110		
46	144	181	ii² 112	290	
47	145	182	iv 556	292	
48	146	180	ii² 114		
49	147	184	ii² 116	293	
50	150	194			
51	151		ii² 126	303	

W/V	Tod, GHI	SIG³	IG	Bengtson	Other
52	153	190	ii² 124	304	
53	154	191	ii² 125		
54	152	193	xii (7) 5		
55	156	192	ii² 123		
56			ii² 404		
57	157	196	ii² 127	309	
58	158			308	
59	159	197	ii² 128	312	
60	160	201	vii 2418		
61	162		ii² 1128	320	
62	163	212	xii (2) 3		
63	165	229		322	
64	166		ii² 211		
65	167	206	ii² 212		
66	168	205	ii² 213	328	
67					Demosthenes 19.19-24
68	169	244 A-E			
69					Speusippos' *Letter to Philip*
70	172	230			
71	173	228	ii² 226		
72	175	256	ii² 233		
73	176		ii² 5226		
74	177	260	ii² 236		
75					*Hesperia* 21 (1952) p. 355
76				210, 233, 261, 344	

INDEX OF PERSONS

Persons appearing only as patronymics are not listed.
"Archon" = "archon at Athens," unless otherwise indicated.

Aeschines, Athenian politician 92, 93, 105
Agaision 69
Agasiklees 42
Agasikratos 102
Agatharchos 71, 73
Agathokles, archon 357/6 77, 80
Agathonymos 97
Agelaos, archon of Thessalian League 74
Agelaos, Ainianian 102
Agesilaus, King of Sparta 6, 7, 9, 15, 16, 17, 22, 32, 35, 44, 48, 56, 100
Agesinikos 85
Agesipolis, King of Sparta 34, 35
Aglaokritos 69
Agyrrhios, Athenian politician 3
Ainesidemos 67
Aischylos 45
Aischylos, archon at Delphi 66, 67
Aischylos of Selinous 66
Aisimos, Athenian politician 8, 35, 37
Aitondas, Boeotarch 59, 65
Aleuas Thorax of Larisa 98
Alexander I of Macedon (ca. 495-450 B.C.) 98, 99
Alexander II of Macedon (369-368 B.C.) 52, 60
Alexander III of Macedon — the Great (336-323 B.C.) 103, 106, 107
Alexander the Molossian 103
Alexander of Pherai 59, 60, 73, 74, 75, 82, 101
Alexandros, Ionian arbitrator 28
Alketas the Molossian 40, 47, 103
Alkibiades, Athenian general 33, 100
Alkimachos from Angele 36
Alkimachos from Anagyrous 77
Alkyoneus, tyrant of Pallene 99
Amadokos, Thracian King 76
Aminadas, Boeotarch 65
Amyntas, King of Macedon 25, 26, 27, 52, 53, 100
Andokos 66
Androkleidas 11, 12, 13
Andron of Athens 87
Andron of Megara 66
Androsthenes 25
Androtion, Atthídographer 79, 89, 90, 91
Aneritos 102
Angeles 28
Antagoras 102
Antalkidas, Spartan commander 29, 30, 32, 33

119

Antenor, Macedonian envoy 52
Antimachos, Athenian Amphictyon at Delos 41
Antimachos, Athenian captain 43
Antimachos, Athenian ambassador 82
Antimachos of Chios 38
Antimachos of Herakleia in Trachis 102
Antipatros of Delos 42
Antipatros of Keos 69
Antipatros of Magnesia 97, 99, 100, 101
Antiphanes 22
Antitheos 11
Anytos, Athenian politician 8
Aphrodite 24
Apollo 41, 46, 57, 66, 68, 75, 83, 84, 85, 86, 93, 99, 101
Apollodoros from Acharne, son of Pasion 53, 54
Apollodoros of Delos 42
Apollonios 89, 90, 91
Aratos of Tenedos 104
Archedemos 80
Archelaidas 9
Archelas 35
Archestratos 53
Archidamos, King of Sparta 31, 58
Archippos 74
Archon, archon at Delphi 94, 95
Ares 82, 106
Ariaios 14
Aristandros 95
Aristaichmos 54
Aristarchos, *prytanis* in Phokaia 27
Aristeides of Tenos 43
Aristippides 28
Aristodemos of Naxos 66
Aristodemos, father of Herakleidai 99
Aristokleides 67
Aristokles 54
Aristomachos, trierarch 99
Aristomachos of Torone 38
Ariston of Delos 42
Ariston of Delphi 102

Ariston, Theban archon 85
Aristophon 68
Aristoteles from Marathon 38, 39, 40
Aristoteles from Acharne 40
Aristotle the philosopher 88
Arkos Teireios 85
Arlissis 63
Arybbas the Molossian 103
Artaxerxes II, King of Persia (404-359 B.C.) 29, 30, 31, 32, 33, 50, 57, 63
Artaxerxes III, King of Persia (359-338 B.C.) 63, 64
Artemis 83
Artemon of Klazomenai 28
Artisyleos 42
Asandros 102
Asias, Theban politician 11
Asopodoros, Boeotarch 65
Aspetos 104
Asteios, archon 373/2 B.C. 55
Astyphilos 37
Athanogeiton 96
Athena 4 (Plate), 34, 39, 41, 69, 71, 82, 88, 89, 90, 106
Athenagores 28
Athenodoros 85

Baton 28
Berisades, Thracian King 76, 81
Brasidas, Spartan commander 52
Bryon 35

Chabrias, Athenian general, 54, 68, 77, 80
Chairestratos 107
Chairon 74
Charattes, regent of Ambrakia 99
Chares, Athenian general 71, 81, 83
Charikleides from Myrrhinous 54
Charikleides, archon 363/2 68, 70
Charikles 70
Charinos from Athmone 39
Charisandros, archon 376/5 41, 43
Charops 85

Cheirikrates 13, 17
Chelonion 21
Choirikos 102
Conon, Athenian general 7, 8, 9, 10, 11, 13, 14, 15, 24, 25, 44, 50
Cyrus, satrap of Lydia 6, 14, 48

Daitadas 102
Damastes the historian 98
Damon 102
Damothenis 67
Damoxenos, archon at Delphi 94, 95
Darius, King of Persia 21
Deiklos 28
Deinias 54
Deinomenes 102
Demainetos of Athens 7, 8, 9
Demainetos of Naxos 66
Demeter 46, 69, 71
Demetrios 69
Democracy 107, 108 (Plate)
Demoklees 22
Demokleides 35
Demokrates of Lamia 102
Demokrates of Lebedos 28
Demomeles 54
Demophilos 62
Demos (the Athenian People) 107, 108 (Plate)
Demosthenes of Boeotia 24
Demosthenes of Neapolis 84
Demosthenes the orator 53, 89, 92, 97, 104, 105
Derkyllidas, Spartan commander 6, 16
Dexileos, Athenian cavalryman 22, 23 (Plate)
Diagoras of Rhodes 11
Dicholeos 28
Dieitrephes, archon 384/3 34
Dikaios, regent of Phyllis 99
Diodoros from Skambonidai 41
Diodotos from Angele 80
Diogiton, Boeotarch 65
Diokles 77
Dion of Alyzeia 85

Dionysios of Byzantium 85
Dionysios I of Syracuse 25, 32, 50, 60, 61, 63, 100, 101, 109, 110
Dionysios II of Syracuse 109
Diophantos, archon 395/4 24
Diophantos of Athens 61
Dioskourides 84
Dioteles 59
Diotimos 80
Dorimachos 10

Earth 82, 83, 106
Echenike 67
Echetimos of Delphi 102
Echetimos of Ioulis 68, 69
Elpines, archon 356/5 81, 84
Epameinondas, Theban general 50, 58, 60, 61, 65, 71, 74, 75
Epicharmos of Arcadia 67
Epigenes, archon at Delos 377/6 41
Epigenes, Athenian ambassador 63
Epigenes, Athenian amphictyon at Delos 41
Epikrates, Athenian amphictyon at Delos 41
Epikrates, Athenian politician 8
Epikrates of Erythrai in Ionia 28
Epikratidas 102
Episthenes 43
Erinyes 71, 73
Euaion 28
Euboulides, archon 394/3 21, 22, 24, 25
Euchares 45
Eudelos 22
Euermos 28
Eukleides, archon 403/2 3
Eukrates of Athens 107
Eukrates of Delphi 95, 96
Eumaridas, Boeotarch 59
Euphrosynos 87
Eurylochos 102
Euthios 54
Eudamos 66
Euktemon 54
Eurybios 66

Eurydika 66
Euteles 67
Evagoras, King of Salamis in Cyprus 25, 29
Exekestides, Athenian politician 36, 74, 77

Galaios, archon at Delos 376/5 43
Glauketos 42
Glaukon 68
Gnathios 21
Grabos the Illyrian 81
Gyes, a Persian 17

Hagnias 8
Hegemon (origin unknown) 67
Hegemon of Byzantium 36
Hegesandros 80
Hegisippos 78
Hekatomnos, father of Maussollos 63, 64
Hera 4 (Plate)
Herakleides of Delphi 102
Herakleides of Ioulis 68, 69
Herakles 73, 98, 99, 101
Hermeias of Atarneus 88
Hermes 83
Herodotos, the historian 98
Herogeiton 28
Hestiaios 36
Hieronymos 10
Hierophon 54
Hippias, Boeotarch 65
Hippias, archon at Delos 375/4 41, 43
Hippodamas, archon 375/4 41, 43, 44
Hippokoon, tyrant of Sparta 99

Idiotes 41
Iphikrates, Athenian general 29, 57, 76, 77
Ismenias, Theban politician 11, 12, 13
Isocrates the orator 97, 98, 99, 100
Isthmerios 28

Jason of Pherai 40, 46, 47, 48, 59, 73, 75

Kalleas, archon 377/6 41
Kallias from Oe 3
Kallibios from Paiania 39
Kallikrates 104
Kalliphantos 69
Kallippos from Aixone 54
Kallisthenes, mover of No. 57 81
Kallistogeiton 84
Kallistratos, Athenian politician 50, 54
Kephalion 55
Kephalos, Athenian politician 8, 33, 35
Kephisodotos, Athenian politician 62
Kephisodotos, sculptor 49
Kephisophon, Athenian politician 3, 5
Kerkinos 85
Kersebleptes, Thracian King 32, 76, 89, 92, 104
Ketriporis, Thracian King 81, 82
Kinesias, mover of No. 11 25
King of Persia 14, 15, 19, 28, 29, 30, 31, 32, 33, 34, 35, 36, 38, 39, 41, 48, 49, 58, 59, 72, 73, 83, 101, 106
Kleandros 102
Kleidas 99
Kleinias of Lebedos 28
Kleino 67
Kleitarchos of Delos 42
Kleogenes 67
Kleombrotos, King of Sparta 44, 57, 58
Kleomenes the Ainianian 102
Kleon, archon at Delphi 102
Kleon of Delphi 96
Kleon of Sikyon 35
Kleoniko 67
Kleotimides 55
Koiratadas, Theban politician 12
Kolonos, *prytanis* in Mytilene 27

Kolosimmos of Thessaly 94, 102
Kombos 66
Kore 71
Koroibos of Sparta 60, 61
Kottabos 66
Kottyphos of Thessaly 94, 102
Kotys, Thracian King 76
Kresphontes, King of Messene 99
Kritios 44
Ktesippos 28
Kteson 67
Kydon 36

Ladikes, regent of Ambrakia 99
Leochares from Pallene 54
Leontiades, Theban politician 12
Leonymos 15
Leophon 42
Leptines 25
Leukinos 42
Leukon, King of Bosporos 87, 89, 90, 91
Lygdamos of Tragila 66
Lyppeios the Paionian 81
Lysander, Spartan commander 3, 17, 18, 19, 20, 29
Lysias from Pithos 81, 84
Lysikrates, shipwright 54
Lysikrates from Oinoe 82
Lysimachos from Acharne 90, 91
Lysippos, the sculptor 60
Lysitheos 22
Lysixenos 66

Malekidas, Boeotarch 65
Manitas 64
Mardonios, Persian commander 98
Maussollos, satrap of Caria 63, 64, 79, 83
Megabates, a Persian 16
Melesias, Athenian cavalryman 22
Menelaos the Pelagonian 70, 71
Menes 77
Menestratos from Aixone 107
Menestratos of Byzantium 36
Menexenos 68

Menon, Boeotarch 59
Menon from Potamos 77
Miltiades 69
Milon 8, 9
Mixias, Boeotarch 65
Mnasidamos 102
Mnasilaos 58
Mnesarchos 81
Mnesilochos 102
Molon, archon 362/1 71, 73
Monounios 81
Moschos 61

Nausigenes, archon 368/7 61
Nausinikos, archon 378/7 39, 40
Neleus, father of Nestor 99
Neokleides 22
Neoptolemos the Molossian 40, 103
Nestor, regent of Messene 99
Nikodemos of Argos 95
Nikolaos 85
Nikoleos 68
Nikomachos 22
Nikon 102
Nikophemos, archon 361/0 74
Nikophemos, assistant to Conon 10
Nikostratos 68, 70
Nobas of Carthage 59
Nymphodoros 28

Oiniades 43
Olympias, mother of Alexander the Great 103
Olympion 102
Onetorides 22
Onomarchos, Phokian general 94, 96
Orthoboulos 36

Pairisades, King of Bosporus 89, 90
Pandion, Athenian hero 65
Pandios of Athens, cavalryman 22
Pandios of Athens, proposer of No. 38 61
Pankalos 17
Pankon 67
Pantaretos 40

Paramythos 61
Parmeniskos 85
Pasion, wealthy Athenian freedman 53
Pasiphernes 14
Patroklees 42
Patron, Boeotarch 59
Pausanias, King of Sparta 3, 20, 34, 35
Peace (Eirene) 49, 51 (Plate), 52
Peisianax 81, 82
Peisios 67
Pelopidas, Theban general 59, 60, 75
Perdikkas III, King of Macedon 70, 75, 100
Periandros, mover of No. 46 71
Phaidros 91
Phaikos 102
Phanes 22
Phanokritos of Parion 33
Phanon 28
Phanostratos 54
Pharax 8
Pharnabazos, satrap of Phrygia 8, 9, 13, 15, 16, 17, 24
Phegon 66
Philinos of Athens 54
Philinos of Byzantium 36
Philinos of Delphi 102
Philip II, King of Macedon 46, 52, 65, 75, 76, 82, 83, 89, 92, 93, 97, 101, 102, 103, 104, 105, 106, 107
Philippos of Athens 73
Philippos of Athens, deme Kolonos 54
Philippos of Athens, deme Semachidai 62
Philittios 68
Philochares 77
Philokles 44
Philokrates, Athenian politician 92, 93
Philomelos, Phokian general 94, 96
Philon 75
Philonautas 102
Philostratos 67

Phoibidas, Spartan commander 35, 37
Phormo 85
Phrynichos, archon 337/6 107
Phylakos 44
Phylarchos, Athenian cavalryman 22
Pistokrates 54
Pistoxenos 42
Plato the philosopher 97, 100, 109
Platon 25
Pleisteas 102
Pollis 9, 13
Polydamas of Pharsalos 46, 47, 48
Polyeuktos 84, 91
Polykles of Athens 54
Polykles of Ephesos 28
Polyxenos 25
Polyzelos, archon 367/6 62
Poseidon 69, 82, 83, 99, 106
Poses of Samos 5
Praxion 95
Prophetes 62
Prothoos of Laconia 57
Ptolemy, Macedonian envoy 52
Pylios, adoptive father of Herakles 98
Pyrrhandros 36, 40
Pythagoras of Naukratis 66
Pythes 28
Pythodoros the Achaian 102
Pythokleides 28
Python of Athens 3, 5
Python of Delos 43

Rhathenes, Persian commander 16
Rhysiades 45

Saraukos 66
Satyridos 69
Satyros of Athens 70, 71
Satyros of Ioulis 68
Satyros, king of the Bosporos 90
Seuthes, Thracian king 32
Simalos 80
Simichos 8
Simon 37

Sithon, regent of Pallene 99
Sodamos 102
Sosibios 66
Sosigenes 41
Sosis of Athens 90
Sosis of Byzantium 85
Sostratos 28
Spartokos, king of the Bosporos 89, 90
Speusippos, nephew of Plato 97
Sphodrias, Spartan commander 35, 37, 44
Spithridates, a Persian 16, 17
Stephanos from Euonymon 53
Stephanos 37
Stephanos 91
Stratokles 75
Strombon 66
Strouses, satrap of Ionia 28, 29
Sun 82, 83, 106
Syleus 99

Teisandros, archon 414/3 22
Teledamos 95
Telegonos 99
Telesegoros 8
Telesikrates 66
Teleutias, brother of Agesilaus 35
Theaitetos 75
Theangelos 22
Thearides 25
Thebagoras, archon at Delphi 96
Themistokles, archon 347/6 90, 91
Theodoros 67
Theodosios 90
Theogenes 86
Theognetos 42
Theokydes 42
Theomnastos 102
Theophilos 90, 91
Theophrastos, archon 340/39 104
Theopompos 38
Theopompos of Thebes 58

Theopompos of Chios, the historian 100
Theoxenos 54
Theudoros 28
Thibron, Spartan commander 6
Thion, Boeotarch 59
Thrason 82
Thrasyboulos from Kollytos 40
Thrasyboulos from Steiria 8, 29
Thrasyboulos of Thespiai 67
Thyssos 64
Timeas 67
Timokrates of Rhodes 8
Timokrates from Krioa 53, 54
Timolaos of Corinth 8
Timoleon, liberator of Sicily 109
Timon, Boeotarch 59
Timondas 102
Timotheos from Anaphlystos 54
Timotheos, Athenian general 50, 52, 70, 100
Timoxenos 69
Tiribazos, satrap of Ionia 29, 32
Tissaphernes, satrap of Caria 9
Tithraustes, satrap of Caria 13, 14, 15
Tmolos 99
Twelve Gods 71, 73
Tyndareus, regent of Sparta 99

Wealth (Ploutos) 50, 51 (Plate)

Xanthippos from Herme 71
Xenodokos 36
Xenodoros 95, 96
Xenokles of Sparta 9
Xenokles, shipwright 54
Xenokrates 58
Xerxes, King of Persia 98

Zenis 28
Zeus 39, 46, 58, 69, 71, 82, 106

GEOGRAPHICAL INDEX

Athenian demes are not listed.

Abdera (in Thrace) 40
Achaia 18, 71, 72, 99, 102
Aegospotami 3, 7, 33
Aetolia 46, 62
Aigina 8, 9, 44, 50
Ainianians 102
Ainos (in Thrace) 40
Akanthos (in Chalcidice) 26
Akarnania 38, 40, 44, 45
Akraiphnia (in Boeotia) 11
Akragas (in Sicily) 109, 110
Alyzeia (in Akarnania) 84, 85
Ambrakia 99
Amorgos 40, 79
Amphipolis 8, 25, 26, 52, 70, 75, 76, 82, 92, 99, 101
Amphissa 105
Anaktorion 84, 85
Andros 40, 79, 80
Anthemos (in Chalcidice) 82
Antissa (on Lesbos) 40
Apollonia (in Illyria) 67
Arcadia 18, 34, 46, 65, 66, 67, 71, 72
Arethousa (in Chalcidice) 40
Argos 7, 8, 12, 18, 19, 29, 30, 34, 35, 72, 95, 102
Arkesine (on Amorgos) 79
Astraiousa (location uncertain) 40
Atarneus (in Aeolis) 88
Athenai (in Euobia) 40
Athens 3, 5, 6, 7, 8, 12, 17, 18, 19, 20, 21, 22, 24, 25, 26, 29, 30, 31, 32, 33, 34, 36, 37, 38, 39, 40, 41, 44, 45, 46, 48, 49, 50, 52, 53, 56, 58, 60, 61, 62, 64, 65, 67, 68, 69, 70, 71, 72, 73, 75, 76, 77, 78, 79, 80, 81, 82, 84, 86, 87, 89, 90, 91, 92, 93, 97, 98, 101, 102, 103, 104, 105, 107, 109
Attica 9, 12, 39, 50, 72, 78
Aulis (in Boeotia) 12

Black Sea 17
Boeotia 7, 8, 11, 12, 13, 17, 19, 20, 24, 30, 34, 37, 44, 48, 50, 56, 57, 58, 59, 93, 105
Bottiaia (in Macedon) 26
Byzantium 27, 36, 40, 65, 79, 84, 85, 105

Camarina (in Sicily) 109
Cappadocia 17
Caria 15, 63
Carthage 59, 109, 110
Chaironeia (in Boeotia) 11, 105, 106
Chalcidice 25, 26, 27, 35, 99
Chalkis (in Chalcidice) 40
Chalkis (on Euboia) 21, 38, 40, 41, 77
Chersonese 76, 92, 104
Chios 3, 28, 34, 35, 36, 38, 39, 40, 79, 83, 88
Cilicia 9, 17
Corcyra 38, 40, 44, 45, 56
Corinth 7, 8, 12, 18, 19, 20, 22, 24, 29, 30, 34, 95, 99, 106
Crimea 87
Cyclades 44
Cyprus 14, 15, 30
Cyrene (in Africa) 100

Daskyleion 17
Daulis (in Phokis) 13
Decelea (in Attica) 8, 12, 14, 33
Delos 25, 41, 42, 43
Delphi 35, 66, 67, 83, 84, 85, 92, 93, 94, 95, 99, 101, 102, 103
Dians from Thrace 40
Dikaiopolis (in Thrace) 40
Dion (in Chalcidice) 40, 83
Dolopes (in Central Greece) 47, 102
Dorians 101, 102
Dryopes 99

Elaious (in the Chersonese) 40
Egypt 50, 54, 66
Elatea (in Phokis) 13
Eleusis (in Attica) 6, 98
Elis 18, 58, 71, 72
Ephesos (in Ionia) 5, 27, 28
Epirus 47, 103
Eresos (on Lesbos) 40
Eretria (on Euboia) 21, 40, 77, 78, 99
Erythrai in Boeotia 11, 12
Erythrai in Ionia 28, 88
Euboia 20, 21, 40, 41, 77, 78, 81, 82, 92
Eurotas River (in Laconia) 58
Eutresis (in Boeotia) 11

Gaetae 25
Gela (in Sicily) 109
Gordion (in Phrygia) 16

Haliartos (in Boeotia) 11, 20, 35
Halykos River (in Sicily) 109, 110
Hellespont 15, 17, 24, 33
Herakleia (in Trachis) 22, 102
Hestiaia (on Euboia) 40, 77
Himera (in Sicily) 109
Hyampolis (in Phokis) 13

Iasos (in Caria) 27
Ikaros 42
Ikos 40
Illyria 25, 26, 81, 98
Imbros 30
Ionia 3, 6, 21, 28, 102
Ios 42
Ioulis (on Keos) 40, 68, 69, 96, 87

Karpasia (on Cyprus) 14, 15
Karthaia (on Keos) 40, 68, 69, 86
Karystos (on Euboia) 40, 77, 78
Kaunos (in Caria) 9, 10, 11, 13, 14, 15
Kelainai (in Phrygia) 10
Keos 40, 42, 55, 68, 69, 70, 80, 86

Kephallenia 38, 40, 44, 45
Kios (in Mysia) 17
Kirrha (in Phokis) 84, 97, 99
Klazomenai (in Ionia) 28, 30
Knidos (in Caria) 7, 24, 27, 29, 44, 105
Kopai (in Boeotia) 11
Koresos (on Keos) 40, 86
Koroneia (in Boeotia) 11, 22, 24, 29
Kos 79, 83
Krenides (in Thrace) 81, 82
Kynoskephalai (in Thessaly) 60
Kypharra (in central Greece) 66
Kythera 24
Kyzikos 16, 17, 27

Laconia 22, 24, 58, 99
Lamia (in Thessaly) 102
Larisa (in Thessaly) 66
Lebadeia (in Boeotia) 11
Lebedos (in Ionia) 28
Lechaion 97
Lemnos 30
Leontinoi (in Sicily) 20, 109
Lesbos 27
Leuktra (in Boeotia) 35, 40, 57, 58, 59, 60, 65, 105
Lilybaion (in Sicily) 109
Lionheads (in Phrygia) 16
Lokris 13, 20, 21, 22, 102
Lydia 10, 15

Macedon 25, 26, 35, 46, 48, 52, 70, 71, 73, 75, 76, 81, 88, 92, 99, 105, 106, 107
Maiandros River 10, 28
Magnesia (in Thessaly) 97, 102
Malians (in central Greece) 102
Mantineia (in Arcadia) 34, 35, 65, 71, 72, 74, 105
Marakoi (in central Greece) 47
Marathon (in Attica) 21
Marganon (in Elis) 58
Maroneia (in Thrace) 40
Matropolis 102
Megara 66

Mende (in Chalcidice) 26
Messana (in Sicily) 109
Messene 99
Messenia 14, 60, 66
Methymna (on Lesbos) 36, 37, 40
Miletos (in Caria) 28
Miletos' Wall (in Phrygia) 17
Molossi 40, 103, 109
Mykonos 40, 42
Mylasa (in Caria) 63, 64
Mysia 15, 16, 17
Mysian Olympos 15, 17
Mytilene (on Lesbos) 3, 27, 36, 38, 40, 87, 88, 91
Myus (in Caria) 28

Naxos 44, 66, 105
Naucratis 54, 66
Neapolis (Neopolis; in Thrace) 40, 83, 84
Nellos (on Zakynthos?) 40
Nemea 22
Notion (in Ionia) 5

Oinaians from Ikaros 42
Oropos (in Attica/Boeotia) 92, 93
Olympia 103
Olynthos (in Chalcidice) 35, 52, 70, 76, 82, 83, 89, 98
Orchomenos (in Boeotia) 11, 17, 20

Paionia 81
Pallene (in Chalcidice) 40, 99
Panormos (in Sicily) 109
Paphlagonia 16, 17
Parapotamia (in Phokis) 13
Parion 33
Parnassos (in Phokis) 13
Paros 40, 42, 55
Pedia (in Phokis) 13
Pelagonia (in Macedon) 70
Peiraieus 7, 18, 24, 35, 37, 44
Peparethos 40
Perinthos 40
Perrhaibians (in central Greece) 102
Persia 6, 7, 12, 14, 24, 39, 41, 48, 49, 50, 56, 72, 88, 101
Phanotea (in Phokis) 13
Pharsalos (in Thessaly) 22, 46, 47, 48, 66
Phaselis 67
Pherai (in Thessaly) 46, 59, 73, 82
Philippi (in Thrace) 81, 83
Phlegyai 99
Phleious (Phlius) 67, 71, 72
Phoenicia 9, 17
Phokaia (in Aeolis) 27
Phokis 11, 13, 17, 22, 56, 57, 82, 84, 92, 99, 101, 103
Phrygia 10, 16, 17
Phthiotians (in central Greece) 102
Phyllis (in Thrace) 99
Plain of Thebe and Apia (in Phrygia) 15
Plataia (in Boeotia) 11, 93, 98
Poteidaia (in Chalcidice) 73, 82, 99
Potniai (in Boeotia) 12
Priene (in Caria) 10
Pronnoi (on Kephallenia) 40

Rhegion (in Italy) 20
Rheneia (near Delos) 43
Rhodes 10, 11, 13, 14, 27, 36, 40, 79, 83

Salamis (in Cyprus) 25, 29
Samos 3, 5, 27, 29, 64, 65
Samothrace 40
Sangarion (in Paphlagonia) 17
Sardis (in Lydia) 9, 29
Schoinos (in Boeotia) 12
Segesta (in Sicily) 109
Selinous (in Sicily) 66, 109, 110
Selymbria (in Thrace) 40
Serdaioi (in Italy) 19
Seriphos 42
Sicily (25, 61), 109, 110
Sikans (in Sicily) 109
Sikels (in Sicily) 110
Sikinos 40
Sikyon (in Achaia) 60
Sinope (in Paphlagonia) 17

Siphnos 40, 42
Skaphai (in Boeotia) 11, 12
Skiathos 40
Skillous (in Elis) 58
Skolos (in Boeotia) 11, 12
Sparta 3, 5, 7, 8, 9, 12, 13, 14, 15,
    17, 18, 19, 20, 22, 24, 25, 26, 27,
    29, 30, 31, 32, 33, 34, 35, 36, 37,
    38, 39, 41, 44, 46, 47, 48, 49, 50,
    52, 56, 57, 58, 60, 61, 66, 67, 71,
    82, 84, 98, 99, 100, 105, 106
Strymon River (in Thrace) 25, 75
Sybaris (in Italy) 19
Syracuse (in Sicily) 25, 50, 61, 66,
    83, 101, 109, 110
Syros 42
Skyros 30

Tanagra (in Boeotia) 11
Tauromenion (in Sicily) 110
Tegea (in Arcadia) 35, 95
Tenos 40, 42
Tenedos 84, 85, 104

Thasos 8, 40, 83
Thebes (in Boeotia) 7, 11, 12, 13,
    17, 19, 20, 27, 30, 34, 35, 37, 38,
    39, 40, 44, 46, 49, 50, 55, 56, 57,
    58, 59, 60, 61, 65, 67, 71, 73, 74,
    77, 79, 82, 84, 92, 93, 101, 105
Thera 100
Thermaians from Ikaros 42
Thespiai (in Boeotia) 11, 67, 93
Thessaly 22, 46, 47, 48, 49, 59, 60,
    73, 74, 75, 92, 97, 98, 101, 102
Thisbai (in Boeotia) 11
Thorikos (in Attica) 9
Thrace 25, 40, 75, 76, 81, 83, 98,
    104
Torone (in Chalcidice) 99
Tragila (in Chalcidice) 66
Trichoneion (in Aetolia) 63
Triphylia (in Elis) 58
Troizen 66

Zakynthos 40, 50